A Giant Among Giants

RABBI SHMUEL KALMAN MELNICK.

A Giant Among Giants

*A History of Rabbi Shmuel Kalman Melnick
and the Princelet Street Synagogue*

by

Samuel C. Melnick

The Pentland Press Limited
Edinburgh · Cambridge · Durham

© S.C. Melnick 1994

First published in 1994 by
The Pentland Press Ltd.
1 Hutton Close
South Church
Bishop Auckland
Durham

All rights reserved.
Unauthorised duplication
contravenes existing laws.

ISBN 1 85821 114 X

Cover: The author with his wife and daughter in the Princelet Street Synagogue (Permission of ES Magazine).

Typeset by Elite Typesetting Techniques, Southampton.
Printed and bound by Antony Rowe Ltd., Chippenham.

Contents

	Foreword	vii
	Introduction	ix
Chapter 1	The Origins of Rabbi Melnick and his Life in Poland	1
Chapter 2	Rabbi Melnick in London	6
Chapter 3	The Death of Rabbi Melnick and his Legacy	26
Chapter 4	History of the Princes Street Synagogue to 1893	36
Chapter 5	Cheap Marriages	58
Chapter 6	The Building Reconstructed	73
Chapter 7	The Early Twentieth Century	89
Chapter 8	The Synagogue in the Mid-Twentieth Century	101
Chapter 9	A Review of a Century of the Princelet Street Synagogue	111
Appendix i	A Humble *Chevra* Room	118
Appendix ii	*Hesped* on the Death of Rabbi Shmuel Kalman Melnick	120
Appendix iii	Translation of the Inscription on Rabbi Melnick's Tombstone	123
Appendix iv	Translations of notes found in some of his books	124
Appendix v	Amalgamation proposal 1952	129
Appendix vi	Elevation of building	130
Appendix vii	Appeal 1892/3	131
	Glossary	132

Foreword

During the war years we left our house in Wilkes Street, Spitalfields and went to live in Letchworth. This small town in Hertfordshire had then a sizeable Jewish community, several thousand Jews having found refuge there during those difficult and troubled times.

In the beginning of 1949 we returned to Wilkes Street. Spitalfields then still contained in its numerous narrow streets scores of small synagogues; Wilkes Street itself had two. The largest of these was the Spitalfields Great or Machzike Hadass; however, tucked away behind the façade of a house in Princelet Street was the oldest of them all. This narrow street was in the heart of the then Jewish district, which at first glance looked very ordinary with no pretence to fame. Nevertheless it contained this beautiful little synagogue and also the house where the late Rabbi Kook (זצ"ל) first Chief Rabbi of Palestine lived. In contrast it was also the home in the nineteenth century of the first Jewish theatre in London founded by Jacob Adler.

At that time the President of the synagogue was Dr Barst, a medical doctor of the old school with a practice in Wilkes Street. He had been our family doctor since my earliest recollections of childhood, who visited us when we were indisposed. Together with Mr Reback, he approached my father (זצ"ל) to become reader/minister of the synagogue in 1950. My father Rev. Noach Kaplin had been born in Jerusalem and came to London before the first World War. He was very active in Jewish education and other affairs. For many years he was the chairman of the Spitalfields Sinai group and also founder member of many youth and charitable institutions. He remained in the position until 1957 when he left to take up a post with the Stepney Orthodox Synagogue.

Most of the small synagogues and many of the streets have disappeared in the ill-advised reconstruction of the district. One of the only ones to survive was the Princelet Street Synagogue, having been built between two early Georgian houses. Little did anyone think then that nearly the only survivor of all these small synagogues would one day become a museum to the glorious past of East London Jewry. Yet that is what has happened and now Samuel Melnick has presented us with a detailed account of those years together with a biography of its longest serving and most illustrious rabbi, his own grandfather.

The book records in detail the congregational life of the synagogue and its various societies in parallel with the life of the author's grandfather, the saintly Rabbi Melnick. Most of its members came from Eastern Europe as he had done, had settled in London free from pogrom and persecution, yet retained their allegiance to their religion and to their community, often maintaining the customs of the country from which they had come. Many events and personalities long forgotten are brought back to life, indeed this so-called minor synagogue is shown to be of considerable historic importance within the Anglo-Jewish community.

Samuel Melnick has not spared time or effort in his research into the not too distant past. He has examined and worked through old papers, minute books, ledgers, newspapers and magazines and has written a fascinating book. This is a faithful record of this synagogue and its rabbi, one which was a prototype of many such synagogues and Chevras in the old East End. I highly recommend this book both to scholars and laymen alike and thank the author for his tremendous work in saving this item of history from oblivion.

Dayan C.D. Kaplin

Introduction

It is possible that Jews first came to England, or rather Britain, in Temple times when Cornwall was the most important source of tin for bronze. Place names such as Mousehole and Marazion suggest such settlements and the name of the well-known beverage from Somerset is a corruption of the Hebrew word for a strong drink. Probably some came in Roman times as both soldiers and slaves to soldiers and there are believed to have been Jewish settlements, but as the Romans went so did the Jews. The first recorded settlements were in the Norman period when many came from France under both William I and II. Several communities, notably in London and East Anglia, were set up and existed, or perhaps survived, until the Jews were expelled from England by Edward I in 1290. Subsequently Jews are recorded as having been in the country for various purposes: mainly, but not entirely, Marranos fleeing the persecution of the inquisition in Spain and Portugal. It was not until 1656 that Oliver Cromwell officially permitted the existence of Jewish communities in the country although this merely gave recognition to an existing situation, some thirty-five families being recorded in 1660. The community grew gradually and at the end of the Napoleonic wars numbered 20,000-30,000, immigration being largely from Central and Eastern Europe. By 1858 when Baron de Rothschild took his seat as Member of Parliament for the City of London after a ten year fight (concerning the wording of the oath) it was about 50,000 and had risen to 60,000 in 1880.

By this time most of the major organisations were in existence. The Chief Rabbi presided over the religious life of the community and five Ashkenazi synagogues had amalgamated in 1870 to form the United Synagogue, subsequently to be joined by others before expanding of its own volition. Kosher meat and poultry were provided by the Board of

Shechita which had been formed in 1804 for both Ashkenazi and Sephardi communities. The Board of Deputies of British Jews represented the community on major occasions and discussed general communal matters; there were various charities catering for the less privileged members of society. In 1887 a large number of smaller synagogues joined forces to form the Federation of Synagogues, an organisation more akin to the needs of the massive immigration taking place at this time, than to the United Synagogue.

Between 1880 and 1905 the number of Jews in England rose dramatically to over 300,000, almost entirely due to Jews fleeing the terror of Alexander III in the lands dominated by Czarist Russia. Those from Northern Europe had journeyed overland to the Baltic ports of Germany, or to Hamburg, and arrived after several days travelling in a dirty and dishevelled condition; from Southern Russia the journey was more complex, usually leaving from Odessa with part overland and part sea voyage. Most had hoped to cross the Atlantic to get to the '*Goldene Medina*' but for various reasons became stranded in England. They carried little luggage and less money. To meet them on the quayside would be some of their co-religionists, missionaries offering food and shelter (and conversion to Christianity) and some less savoury characters out to rob them of what little they might have or to offer young ladies 'some lucrative employment' in the great city. Initially they would be accommodated at the Jews' Temporary Shelter in Leman Street, later in Mansell Street, whose representatives met every ship arriving, until they were able to move on. Most, being craftsmen of some sort, soon found jobs. In the tailoring trade, which accounted for the majority, the more enterprising set up their own businesses while others found work in the sweatshops with long hours and low rates of pay. They did not move far from the port areas and soon, as the Jews moved in, whole streets in which even policemen in pairs preferred not to walk, lost their unsavoury reputations. Meanwhile, in London, Lord Rothschild founded the Four Percent Industrial Dwelling Trust to provide better accommodation for the immigrants at rents they could afford. A new 'ghetto' formed in the East End, almost entirely self-contained with its own shops, synagogues and Hebrew schools. Yiddish was the language of the newcomers and it is doubtful if any could speak English on their arrival; indeed most could not even speak the language of the country from which they came and fewer still could read or write it.

Although this new 'ghetto' was established on the lines of those they had known in Eastern Europe, there was one important difference – all the children had to go to school, usually to the local Board schools where they had to speak English. Many of these schools very soon had almost only Jewish pupils and even the Jewish schools, notably the Jews' Free School in Bell Lane, were more interested in making the youngsters little English men and women than knowledgeable Jews.

The existing community consisted largely of comfortable middle-class families well integrated into the life of the nation. There were Jews in all walks of life, in both Houses of Parliament and the Universities. A Jew, albeit a convert to Christianity, had been Prime Minister and there could have been few who had not heard of Sir Moses Montefiore. Although a closely cohesive group and committed to their religion a large proportion were not deeply involved in its practice. For the most part they were opposed to the immigrants and did their best either to persuade them to return whence they came or to carry on travelling to America or elsewhere.

The new immigrants were poor but hard working and in the main deeply involved in the various practices of the religion although they did number a significant number of anarchists and other anti-religious elements. Their effect, not only on the Jewish community, but on the nation as a whole, was out of all proportion to their numbers. In response to much agitation, immigration controls were introduced in 1906 and, additionally, a number of anti-semitic groups arose. However, these were isolated and the police dealt with any disturbances without favour. Probably the most important effect on the general populace was the arrival in the country of large numbers of skilled tailors and other garment workers. The sudden coming of these workers resulted in the increased manufacture of good quality clothing for both men and women at much lower prices than had hitherto been the case, such now becoming available at prices that working people could afford and they were becoming better dressed. In Leeds a certain Montague Burton opened a low cost bespoke tailoring factory while in the same city Michael Marks set up a chain of stalls known as 'penny bazaars', then moved to Manchester where he was joined by a non-Jew, Tom Spencer. But not all the newcomers were tailors, garment workers or other types of artisan. Among their number were several rabbis and *chazanim* already well established on the Continent. Many of the rabbis were of a calibre as scholars and preachers rarely, if ever, seen this side of the North Sea, and even among them some stood out. It is the purpose of this book to relate the life of one who stood out as sage, preacher and counsellor; to describe the extraordinary scenes attendant upon his demise and to relate the story of the historic synagogue to which he was attached for twenty-four of the thirty-five years he spent in the great metropolis.

But why did they come at all? In the nineteenth century Czarist Russia dominated Eastern Europe and in this area lived the largest concentration of Jews in the world; some 14% of the population of Poland was Jewish and a number of towns were, in effect, entirely Jewish. There were many great scholars, writers and preachers, some household names to this day. The Chassidic movement of today had its origins here, and there were many fine *yeshivot*; Yiddish was the lingua franca of the masses although some scholars might have spoken Hebrew on Sabbath and Festival. Few spoke the language of the country in which they lived.

In 1827 Czar Nicholas I made military service compulsory for Jewish boys aged twelve to eighteen although many as young as eight were recruited. They were stationed in remote parts of the Russian Empire and not allowed to follow their religious practices. Despite the intervention of Sir Moses Montefiore from England the system was not abolished until the accession of Alexander II in 1855. The new Czar made a series of liberal reforms including abolition of the boys' military service but these did not last long and he soon fell back into the ways of his predecessors. In 1863 Poland after some fighting was divided between Russia, Germany and Austria-Hungary. Although much of the oppression fell on the Jews it was by no means confined to them and soon revolutionary groups began to arise. On 1st March 1881 one such group assassinated the Czar. Subsequently six young people were sentenced to death for the deed, although one, a Jewish girl, Khasia Helfman, had her sentence commuted to life imprisonment in the fortress of Petropavlosk. The new Czar Alexander III was no liberal, his reign being characterised by terror and pogroms. (It was this followed by the incompetence of his son Nicholas II which resulted in the revolutions of 1917 and the demise of the Romanoff dynasty.) Conditions deteriorated rapidly with frequent government-inspired attacks on the Jews, the police standing idly by or moving the rioters on to spread the terror. Those who could, sold up in an effort to cross the Atlantic, some three million leaving. About half reached America, with the next largest contingent settling in Great Britain. Others made their way to Argentina or parts of the British Empire, mainly South Africa and Australia, but many never left the European mainland.

The new arrivals in London tended to set up their own places of worship rather than join existing ones; certainly they found nothing in common with the constituents of the United Synagogue. Surprisingly enough few joined even the smaller independent congregations which were immigrant inspired; thus, as we shall see, although small congregations mushroomed in the Spitalfields and Whitechapel areas, the existing ones had to fight for

Introduction xiii

numbers to keep themselves viable, both spiritually and financially. With the passing of time these small groupings slowly amalgamated to provide more suitable units and as the children of the founders merged into the original community and moved away from the East End, a movement accelerated by the second world war, most of these synagogues became redundant and closed. Very few even survive physically, destruction by enemy action and developers having taken their toll. Today some half dozen synagogues exist in an area where, at one time, there were over a hundred and the future of some of these is in doubt. The descendants of these poverty-struck immigrants are now the leading figures in all the major Anglo-Jewish institutions and many hold important positions in all walks of life in the country.

For the benefit of younger readers who have grown up with decimal coinage and pocket calculators I feel it necessary to explain the money system in use during the period covered by the book. One pound was made up of twenty shillings, each in turn consisting of twelve pence annotated as £ s. d. A guinea, at one time a separate coin, was £1 1s. 0d. or twenty-one shillings. Each penny was also divided into halfpence (pronounced ha'pence) and quarters or farthings. Another coin was the half-crown worth two shillings and sixpence (2s. 6d.).

Chapter 1

The Origins of Rabbi Melnick and his Life in Poland

And the L-rd said to Abram, leave for your own sake your country, your birth place, your father's house for a land which I will show you.
(Genesis XII 1)

Arriving by sea at the Baltic port of Gdansk the traveller then motors south along the E81 route towards Warsaw. After some four hundred kilometres, the T81 road from Bydgoszcz is met at a small town named Plonsk. This junction town has a population of about 7,800 and local industries include the manufacture of agricultural machinery, flour milling, timber, brewing and distilling, and clothing manufacture. Before the Nazi invasion of 1939 the Jewish community numbered about 6,000, accounting for almost the entire population. All were deported and the community was not re-established subsequently. An illustration of the Great Synagogue founded in the early seventeenth century appears in the *Encyclopaedia Judaica* although the community itself is listed as having been established in 1446. No doubt there were many other smaller synagogues. Its best known son was David Greenberg, later Ben-Gurion, first Prime Minister of the new State of Israel.

It was here in the early years of the nineteenth century that Tobias Mlynek earned a living as a baker. About 1815, his wife Malka gave birth to a son named Moshe Eli, apparently her only child although there is evidence of an older son, Shlomo Eliezer, who died in 1873. The Civil Registers of Plonsk prior to 1815 are not available and considerable gaps exist among those that are. We do not hear of the family again until 28th February 1836 when Moshe Eli married Chana Leiba, daughter of Faga

Zakroczym, the name of her father not being entered. The entry gives the name of the bride as Chaja Leiba but this, clearly, is an error. In 1839 her first child, Gershon Yaakov, was born, although the birth was not registered for a further three years (a large number of belated registrations in 1842 suggests some sort of a clampdown by the authorities). A second son, Urka; a daughter, Golda; and a third son Judah were born during 1844, 1850 and 1858 respectively. Of Urka and Golda I have no further information. Judah, it appears, married at about the age of thirteen and his first child Faga Rivka was born March 1873. He came to England about the turn of the century with his wife Rachel Leah and family but decided that the supervision of *kashrus* was not up to his standards and eventually returned to Poland, apparently minus at least one daughter, Alta Yocheved who, in the meantime, had married Avram Rudolf. Rachel Leah died in 1914; Judah subsequently returned to London, dying 17th August 1927 (Av 19 5687), and was buried at Edmonton Federation cemetery. Some of his children stayed behind in Poland; at least one grandson survived the Holocaust and is now resident in Israel. But it is the eldest son, Gershon Yaakov, in whom we are mainly interested. As with the other members of the family we know almost nothing of his life. We may assume that he went through the usual educational process of kindergarten, Talmud Torah and *yeshivah*. What we do know is that towards the end of his second decade he journeyed south along what is now that same E81 road to Zakroczym, a small town (population 3,358 in 1970) and port on the river Vistula with principal industries of flour milling and chicory processing. The population in 1892 was 5,500, the entire Jewish community, as in Plonsk and most other towns in Poland, having been deported by the Nazis during the second world war.

The objective of this excursion was matrimony and on 6th February 1860 he married Leah Lichtenstein. The registration records that he was aged twenty and she nineteen. Parental permission for Leah to marry had been obtained and the appropriate announcements had been made in both the Zakroczym and Plonsk synagogues on three successive Sabbaths prior to the event. His occupation was listed as tailor, his father's as chandler; the Lichtensteins were described as traders. The bride's father, Zalman Ber, had died aged thirty-five in 1853, there being one other issue of that marriage, a son, Abraham. The couple set up home in Zakroczym and on 26th November 1862 (Kislev 4th 5623) their first child, a boy, was born. He was named Shmuel Kalman, apparently after Leah's grandfather Shmuel Kalman Prag who had died shortly before the wedding. Subsequently there were three daughters and a second son but owing to the time gap between the fourth and fifth children it is possible that there were others who did not survive. Indeed, the second child, a daughter, Adel, born 1865, was not known to others of the family although her death is not recorded by 1878, the last year for which records are currently available to the public.

From an early age Shmuel Kalman showed considerable academic ability, graduating rapidly from the obligatory kindergarten and Talmud Torah stages to the *yeshivah* whence he studied under Rabbi Yitschok of Jelowa (near Sochuszew), Rabbi Dov Menachem Regensberg of Zimbrova (Governorship of Lomza) and then under Rabbi Yisroel Itsha of Povoznik (near Warsaw). At the age of eighteen and with the wealth of knowledge he had garnered at these academies he returned to his home town to be ordained rabbi by the two rabbis of the town Yisroel Yaakov and Yechiel Michal Haçohen in a mixed written and oral examination lasting a full week. A rider attached to the certificate stated that the examiners expected this young man would become a great rabbi and teacher in Israel. Not content with this he continued his studies under these two and subsequently received a further *semicha* from Rabbi Shlomo Zeidenfeld of Ciechanow. At some time it appears he was seriously ill and in accordance with custom, to enhance recovery was given the additional name of Chaim. In 1882 and still not quite twenty he married Rivka Rachel, third child of Aron and Surah Leah Kazryelovitz and three years his senior. Two older children of this couple, Mordechai and Leiba Dvorah, had died at separate times, aged nine years and eighteen months respectively, during 1859, the same year as the birth of Rivka. The two continued to live in Zakroczym, he earning his living in adult education and as *shochet* whilst continuing studies in law and human relationships resulting in his appointment as a *dayan* both of the local Beth Din and that of Warsaw by the age of twenty-one. But the year was 1884 and Czar Alexander III was well established on the throne with his bitter anti-Jewish campaign of pogroms well under way; the latter appointment, owing to the travelling conditions, could not be sustained and he soon had to resign the position. The first two children were both girls: Rosie Faga born 1883 and Ettie 1889, the gap suggesting others who did not survive. In late 1891 my father who was named Gershon Yaakov was born, indicating that Shmuel Kalman's father had already died (it is the custom among Ashkenaz Jews not to name children after living relatives), and in the two following years another daughter Millie and a son David were added to the family.

But what was life like in those small Polish towns towards the end of the nineteenth century? The Jewish community often represented a very high proportion of urban settlement, in some towns for all practical purposes, the entire population! Houses generally were of wood; brick and stone were rare; usually single-storeyed with two or three rooms although two-storeyed houses were not unknown. Synagogues were also often of wooden construction with lavishly decorated interiors. Water was obtained from a well or, if there was one nearby, a river and in either case had to be boiled on a wood or coal fire in some kind of kitchen range before it was fit to drink. Likewise all cooking would have been on the same kitchen range. Artificial light was from candles or oil lamps (note that Moshe Eli's trade was given as chandler). The usual means of transport was a combination of 'shanks pony' and the horse although steam-driven railways were beginning to be introduced, roads at best being of cobble stones. Most people were poor, obtaining little more than subsistence wages in local industries or the tailoring trade. The Mlynek family was no exception, father being in the tailoring trade and with four children to look after, at least one undergoing advanced education, money was very scarce. Nevertheless Jewish life was vibrant in spite of the conditions; every community had its quota of officials, and houses of learning at all levels abounded. There were writers and musicians, preachers, readers and men of learning. The Rav of the town would concern himself with local problems, assisted by his Beth Din and would consult other rabbanim whenever he felt the need. In general he would preach only twice a year on Shabbat Hagadol and Shabbat Shuva giving a learned discourse on some relevant topic. Routine preaching was normally left to itinerant preachers (*maggidim*), not necessarily qualified rabbis, travelling from town to town.

Shmuel Kalman as a *dayan* made himself a reputation for the humanity of his decisions, a somewhat unusual characteristic of his time, for in general, the rabbis ruled over their flocks with a certain lack of appreciation of the ordinary person's problems. In addition he imbibed the techniques of the *maggidim* to become a more than competent preacher. He was also a competent synagogue reader. A further adjunct of his training was as a *shochet*. Thus did life proceed peacefully if not too happily until late summer 1893 when disaster struck. Timber houses dried out by the summer heat are no barrier to fire and there were no fire brigades with high pressure hoses, etc. to control a conflagration. Much of the town was destroyed and my father often used to talk about it, whether from personal memory, he was not yet two years of age, or from being told about it, I have been unable to devine. Sadly, this was not an uncommon feature in Eastern Europe and references to destruction of whole towns are not infrequent. Not all these fires were accidental and the Jewish quarter usually suffered worse than other parts. Subsequent to news of the fire reaching London some of his former acquaintances wrote inviting him to join them in the capital. Who these were is not known but Rev. Moses Louis Cohen, Reader of the Borough Synagogue and previously of the Princes Street Synagogue and his wife were both natives of Zakroczym and names of others are recorded; also many of his former *yeshiva* colleagues were by this time in London.

To leave your home town, your wife (possibly pregnant) and five children as well as a widowed mother, a young brother and two sisters and go to a foreign country whose language you cannot speak and about which you know almost nothing is a major step in anyone's life. However, after much heart-searching he decided to test the waters and left his family. It is possible that he travelled in the company of Rabbi Elias Regensberg, known as the Meshulach of Lomza and son of one of his teachers. The probable route was overland to Hamburg via Warsaw and Berlin, then by steerage class sea crossing to London. It was 1894, he was aged thirty and had received the promise of a position as general factotum (reader, preacher, teacher, etc.) at the Chevra Poale Zedek, Bnei Suwalk at 58 Hanbury Street in Spitalfields, East London. This tiny synagogue had already been in existence for over ten years and was seeking to join the Federation of Synagogues in order to amalgamate with the Hope Street Synagogue and others to form, in Great Garden Street, one of the new model synagogues envisaged by the Federation of Synagogues. In this respect he was luckier than many for most rabbis (and others for that matter) arrived more in hope than expectation of obtaining remunerative employment.

Chapter 2
Rabbi Melnick in London

You, Whose might is in the heavens and Whose dominion is on earth, have the power to raise up the downtrodden: the righteous shall praise Your name when you raise aloft those who have been purified seven times.
(Penitential prayers for second weekday prior to Rosh Hashanah.)

Rabbi Melnick arrived in London during 1894, probably in time for the High Festivals. On arrival he would have been met by the usual official from the Jews Temporary Shelter in Leman Street and by officers of the synagogue to which he had already been assigned as well as at least some of the friends who had invited him initially. Although accommodation had been obtained for him, no record of the address exists; it must be assumed that it was some kind of lodging. In addition, before being allowed to practise in London, permission from the Chief Rabbi was necessary. Accordingly he was very soon introduced to Dr Hermann Adler whose fiat was readily given. Further, the newcomer was invited to join his select band of outstanding rabbis which met weekly to study some aspect of the codes. But one thing was made clear; in England there was only one rabbi and that was the Chief Rabbi, everyone else was to be '*Reverend*' and was expected to adopt the dress of the Anglican cleric, the Chief Rabbi himself being dressed in the manner of a Bishop. The immigrant rabbis, in general, accepted the downgrading in title but stopped short of changing their manner of dress. The silk top-hat, rather than the shovel hat, was *de rigueur*.

Having come from that part of Poland annexed by Russia there was a problem with the spelling of the name. Although the Polish form Mlynek would be acceptable in English, he appears to have opted for a variation of that or a transliteration of the Russian form so that the spellings Melnik,

Melnick, Melynek, Melinek as well as Mlynek are all to be found. Both Melnick and Melinek were the usual forms and remain so.

The synagogue at 58 Hanbury Street had been in existence since at least 1885 and was a hotbed of the Chavovei Zion, a religious Zionist organisation with the Kamenitzer Maggid, Rabbi Chaim Zundel Maccoby, among its leaders. Although the original building still stands, there is no trace of its part in the history of London Jewry. This is by no means unique for in London's East End: Spitalfields, Whitechapel St. George's in the East, etc., this could be said of many a building. The number of such buildings I have been able to discover runs into three figures and small groups formed *minyanim* which were never recorded or registered anywhere, perhaps in a room in someone's house, perhaps in a couple of rooms especially hired or even a workshop just cleared for the purpose.

There are no press records of his association with this particular synagogue and the only record of it occurs in the book *Oholei Shaim* by Shmuel Noach Gottleib, published in Pinsk 1912. We only read again in the press about the Bnei Suwalk Synagogue of its attempts to join the Federation of Synagogues and amalgamate with the Hope Street (now Wilkes Street) and Eye of Jacob Synagogues in order to form another of the model synagogues projected by that parent organisation. The former objective was achieved in February 1895, the latter not until 30th August 1896 when, with the Wilna Chevra replacing the Eye of Jacob Synagogue, the new building at 9/11 Great Garden Street was opened. Clearly Shmuel Kalman was impressed with Anglo-Jewry and its numerous organisations, Chief Rabbinate, Beth Din, centralised Shechita Authority, charity societies and, above all and in every sense, the United Synagogue. He briefly returned to Poland to bring the family to the new land and obtained accommodation at 138 Davis Mansion Buildings, New Goulston Street. While in this post a fourth daughter, Annie, was born. Pay at the Suwalki was poor and his training as a *shochet* now became valuable for he was able to obtain a position as such with the Board of Shechita. This appears to have been a very senior post, apparently as chief *shochet* of the poultry section and possibly as unofficial deputy to Rabbi Nachum Lipman the Rosh Hashochetim. With six children, the eldest thirteen, space in the flat must have been at a premium let alone with two, or possibly three, other adults although these may have been living elsewhere. One sister may have come with or gone directly to the USA, but she married early the following year. His brother Solomon set up as a tobacconist at 4 Bell Lane and married Rachel Benjamin the following year; their mother went to live with the newly weds.

In late November 1895 Louis Cohen, rabbi of both the Chevra Tehillim Umishmorim of the Princes Street Synagogue and of Mile End New Town Synagogue, Dunk Street died aged about sixty-eight. The account book of the Chevra Tehillim in an entry dated 31st December informs us that Rev. S. Melnik was paid ten shillings for 'services' without any definition of the term. The same source records that on 29th March of the following year he was paid £1 for two week's activities. An advertisement in the *Jewish Chronicle* of 17th April 1896 under the heading '**Chevra Tehillim Umishmorim held at Princes Street Synagogue**' announced that 'Rev. S. Melnik has been duly elected Rabbi to this Society. Tehillim is chanted every Sabbath at 1 p.m. and also expounded by the Rabbi two hours prior to the Evening Service'. A notice of thanks from the rabbi for his election was carried in the next issue; no charge for either item appears in the accounts and it might be interesting to speculate who paid for them. His salary was initially ten shillings per week. Also in connection with this appointment he had an address stamp made in which he describes himself (in Hebrew) as '*maggid* of Princes Street Synagogue and of Old Castle Street Synagogue' suggesting that he was rabbi of two congregations just as was his predecessor. The address on this stamp was 138 Davis Mansions Buildings, New Goulston Street. From this point in time onwards his name appears frequently in the press reporting charity collections and addresses to various organisations and synagogues in addition to Princelet Street.

The first reference to his connection with the Old Castle Street Synagogue was in the *Jewish Chronicle* of 19th March which reported that he had addressed the assembly at a dinner held at the Criterion Hall in Hanbury Street to celebrate the clearance of the debt (from the rebuilding during 1891) of £300. At this same meeting a presentation of an illuminated vellum was made to Mark Moses in appreciation of his twelve years as President of the congregation. (This synagogue had been formed by amalgamation of the Chevra Gemilus Chasodim and Chevra Shalom V'Emeth. The new building was opened during April 1872 in a ceremony conducted by Rev. Guinsburg of Princes Street who also preached the dedication sermon.) In June of that year the diamond Jubilee of Queen Victoria was celebrated and again he is reported as preaching at Old Castle Street, announcements and reports describing him variously as Rev. P., Rev. S., Rev. L. Melnick or Melnik while the *Jewish Chronicle* reported, 'Old Castle Street, the nicest decorated Shule, had a sermon by Rev. M. Melnick; the Rev. L. Weissburg was the reader.' The *Jewish World* described this sermon as impressive.

The birth of yet another daughter, Sarah, in January 1897 appears to have precipitated a change of abode to 5 Princelet Street opposite the synagogue. (This house was renumbered to 10 during 1923 and demolished, together with 6 and 8, prior to the second world war to make way for a clothing factory.) A rubber stamp with the same Hebrew wording as before but with the address as 5 Princelet St., late Princes St., Spitalfields, London, E. was obtained.

One organisation with which he was closely associated was the Foreign Jewish Ladies Benefit Society which, despite its name, seems to have consisted to a large extent of men, although the beneficiaries were women only. He is frequently recorded as delivering speeches at its gatherings and at times chairing the society's meetings. Another organisation of which he was rabbi was the Chevra Ahavath Torah, an offshoot of the Old Castle Street Synagogue, whose first annual gathering received 'a lengthy *drosha*' from its erudite leader. During the same week he opened the proceedings at the Simchat Torah celebrations of the aforementioned synagogue held at Kings Hall, Commercial Road.

In the case of burials of those without synagogue, or at least burial society membership, costs would be paid for out of a charity fund but no form of memorial would be erected under these conditions. Consequently we read in the *Jewish Chronicle* of 12th November that 'Rabbis I. Dainow and S. K. Melnick delivered addresses at the setting of the tombstone to the late Rabbi Isaac Hirschenson at West Ham cemetery, the stone having been presented by Mrs. M. Solomons of New Road and her friends.' (Rabbi Hirschenson had been studying manuscripts at the British Museum in connection with commentaries and periodicals he was editing in Jerusalem and died at the age of forty-six in the Metropolitan Hospital, Kingsland Road, London on 7th October 1896.) Indeed poverty at this time was such that many societies organised for other purposes set up funds to relieve hardship among their members. Thus the *Jewish World* of 10th December reported that the Chevra Ahavath Torah, mentioned above, with membership standing at 120, was to open a fund to pay half a guinea *shiva* benefit to its members for a twopence a week addition to its membership fee.

Another notable event occurred a fortnight later when a new Sepher Torah was consecrated during Chanukah for the Warsaw Synagogue. The first part of the ceremony took place at the Grand Hall, Spital Square where the completion of the writing took place, Rev. Gidenansky conducted the service and Rabbis Lipman and Melnick, Messrs. Osterlinki (President), Z. Diamond and A. Englander delivered addresses. The scroll was then carried in procession to the synagogue in Gun Street, especially decorated for the event.

Early in the new year, 1898, Rabbi Melnick was re-elected rabbi of the Chevra Tehillim, which reported him as 'giving every satisfaction,' a surplus for the year of £71 being reported to the meeting. Two weeks later on Shabbat, 22nd January, he addressed the Stepney Orthodox Synagogue when Harris, eldest son of Mr and Mrs Alexander, celebrated his barmitzvah by reading the entire *sedra*. The 4th February issue of the *Jewish World* carried an item that 'Mr. Davis and Rev. Fassenfeld collected 6s. 6d. for the Great Garden Street Talmud Torah Classes at the wedding of Rev Mlynek's sister'; an event I have been unable to find any record of at either St. Catherine's House or the London Beth Din. It is known that both his sisters settled in the USA and it is possible that the marriage took place there with some celebration being held in London. Alternatively it was a *'stille chasana'* so that no record other than that of the Ketuba ever existed. (The original Polish spelling is also not that unusual for it had been used to register the birth of his youngest daughter only a year earlier.)

What might be termed the ultimate accolade of recognition by the Anglo-Jewish establishment took place on 19th March when, for the first time, he gave the address at the Sabbath afternoon service for Jewish working men and women at the Great Synagogue, Duke Street. (These services were designed for those who through economic necessity or otherwise were forced to work on Sabbath mornings but could attend a service in the afternoon.) A galaxy of major speakers from the various synagogues preached at these services which were also choral although, apart from the Chief Rabbi who always inaugurated each session, only the Yiddish speakers could draw enough people to crowd the building. This, in turn, presented problems because members did not like these 'poor, unkempt foreigners' using their magnificent edifice. On this occasion a large attendance and an elegant sermon were reported but without a mention of its content. Another type of institution in vogue in the East End and out of favour with the 'Establishment' was the Talmud Torah. These were being set up by the new immigrants to provide religious education in out-of-school hours for a very large number of children to an advanced level, the older pupils studying Talmud. An attempt by Lord Rothschild with the support, both tacit and voiced, of the Chief Rabbi to close them and send the children to the Free School in Bell Lane was met with contempt. The movement prospered, if not financially, with larger premises having to be sought from time to time. Classes were held on

Sunday mornings and Monday to Thursday evenings. In August, with Rabbi Melnick as one of the speakers, an appeal was launched for funds for the Commercial Road Talmud Torah, most of whose pupils were from families who could not afford to contribute towards their education.

At some time during this year he was approached, presumably by the Chief Rabbi, to become a *dayan* of the London Beth Din, an appointment which would enhance the standing of that institution. Rabbi Maccoby was also approached, and both for different reasons refused the position: Rabbi Melnick because it would have involved him in preaching at the Great Assembly Hall, Mile End Road and like places which were frequently used by missionaries attempting to convert Jews to Christianity (my father always considered this to have been an error of judgement on his part but, being only about six at the time, was hardly in a position to advise); Rabbi Maccoby because as a vegetarian he felt he could not answer problems on *shechita*. It is possible that others were approached but I have no knowledge of such.

In September he was principal speaker at the presentation of books by Mesdames Isaacs and Harris to the Chevra Shass Synagogue, 26 Old Montague Street, this taking place on the same day as the somewhat delayed official opening of the Spitalfields Great Synagogue by the Chevra Machzike Hadass in a major ceremony properly described elsewhere. His connection with the Chevra Shass did not end there for on Rosh Hashana he is reported as having assisted with its services, a new Ark curtain having been presented by Mrs Guttenburg; additionally he also preached at Princelet Street. On the first day of Succoth he again attended the Chevra Shass, this time as preacher. The winter session appears to have drawn him to speak at a large number of meetings, mainly ladies' societies but at least once at the presentation of boots to poor children.

A notable event was the celebration of the completion of the study of the entire Talmud (*Siyum Hashass*) by Dayan Bernard Spiers on 10th January 1899, coinciding with the *Jahrzeit* of the previous Chief Rabbi, Nathan Adler. The *Jewish Chronicle* reported an outline of the *dayan*'s remarks which were mainly on some aspects of the last tractate, Niddah. The meeting was chaired by the Chief Rabbi and traditional refreshments, punctuated by several speakers, followed. Although listed among those present, Rabbi Melnick was not among the speakers. Finally Dr Friedlander was called upon by acclamation to speak; he stated that he had listened sympathetically to what had been said and would merely reply 'Amen' to their blessing.

Back at Princelet Street the annual 7th Adar service, one of the terms of the merger with the Chevra Mikra, commemorating the death of Moses the Law-giver, was advertised to be addressed by Dayanim Spiers and Sussman Cohen, Rabbis Lipman and Melnick, followed by refreshments at the Criterion Club in Hanbury Street. The *Jewish Chronicle* report of the event a week later listed the speakers as Dayan S. Cohen, Rabbis S. K. Melnick and I. Newman while a banquet, presided over by Philip Silverstone took place at the Criterion, Hackney Road. One year later almost to the week, Rabbi Melnick again addressed the afternoon service at the Great Synagogue, again an eloquent sermon in Yiddish being reported, but once again no content. Pesach that year occurred in late March and for the first time, if only vaguely, a mention of the sermon content was to be found. The *Jewish World* of 31st March under the heading 'East End Passover Services' observed:

> Every seat was occupied and one could scarcely find standing room and although in many cases the service was not over until nearly 1.30 p.m. the worshippers did not leave the sacred building until the last word of prayer had been uttered. Here the Rev. H. Orleansky preached, there it was the Rev. S. K. Melinck and their discourses conveyed words of comfort to those who had escaped from bondage in Russia and were anxious to get to a still freer life in their own land Palestine.

But Rabbi Melnick not only preached during that festival, he also conducted the services, receiving two guineas for his trouble, the reason for the absence of Rev. Fassenfeld not being recorded. At the end of April at the Artillery Lane Synagogue he addressed the Foreign Jewish Ladies Society which, during July, spawned the Ladies Society for Visiting the Sick and Assisting with Funerals of which he became chairman. During the ensuing summer three new synagogues, the New Hambro (off Commercial Road), Fieldgate Street Great, and Spital Square were consecrated and although it was not reported it must be assumed he attended at least one of these. Rosh Hashana that year saw a new departure for him; he addressed the Plotzker Shool which had recently been redecorated, the occasion being marked by the presentation of silver breast plates and bells. (The Plotzker Synagogue had been founded in 1872 by members of the Plotzker Friendly Society who initially used a small room for worship until twenty years later it was able to obtain more suitable premises at the rear of 45 Commercial Road, remaining there until expiration of the lease in 1931 when it amalgamated with the Great Alie Street Synagogue.) The same report also informs us that he officiated and preached at the Lodzer

Shool (5 Davis Mansions, New Goulston Street) both on these days and on Yom Kippur, this time referring to the 'Rennes Verdict' in the Dreyfus case.

Despite the outbreak of the Boer War some months earlier, the final year of the century began with much the same routine as before. His apparently annual contribution to the Sabbath Afternoon addresses at the Great Synagogue was on 27th January when during the course of his homily he pointed out the duties of Jews in time of crisis by personal service or by subscriptions to alleviate the sufferings of those wounded in the war and to help the bereaved of those who had fallen. He also noted that many East End Jews had already personally volunteered for active service. The annual seventh Adar service at Princelet Street took place as usual with Dayanim Spiers and Cohen, Rabbis Lipman and Melnick giving the addresses as advertised. Dayan Spiers noted that this was the 35th time he had attended this event; as time was to prove it was almost his last. For Pesach, Rabbi Melnick 'held forth to a large congregation' (elsewhere described as inconveniently crowded) at the Chevra Shass, Old Montague Street.

During 1899 the Chevra Ahavath Torah was absorbed by the Plotzker Shool and at the Annual meeting the following April Rabbi Melnick was appointed rabbi. (It might be of interest to note at this point that Isaac Kaliski was secretary of this synagogue as well as those of Old Castle Street and Princelet Street and the Chevra Tehillim of both!) (The reader might be amused to learn that the *chazan* of this synagogue was Rev. Shoolsinger.) There is no record of the rabbi terminating his appointment at Old Castle Street but it must be assumed that this was the case.

About this time the family moved house once again, leaving the immediate confines of Spitalfields for St. Georges in the East where they took up residence at 42 Rutland Street (now Ainsworth Road). In June of this same year Mrs Melnick gave birth to her eighth child and third son Nathan of whom more later. During Rosh Hashana our Rabbi addressed the Great Alie Street congregation on the afternoon of the first day and on Shabbat Shuva the Sandys Row Synagogue, again at the afternoon service, this commencing at 1.30 p.m. With Shabbat terminating at 6.23, even allowing for a traditional *Seuda Shelishit* the mind boggles at the length of this traditionally erudite discourse. It is, though, on record that on a number of occasions he spoke for anything up to four hours, usually without notes. He preached there again on Succoth although the report does not detail the time.

By this time he had become popularly known as Reb Shmuel Kalman and it was in this form that the *Jewish World* of 1st February 1901 reported him on the marking of a significant event in British history. It observed:

> Whatever might be wanting in the appearance of the sacred fane (men dressed in black, women soberly, Ark, etc. dressed in black where possible) the maggid made good. Every local preacher whether it was Reb Yitzchok or Reb Shmuel Kalman or the Grodno Maggid felt called upon, either during the morning or the afternoon service to refer to the loss that had been suffered. Men wore black ties and bows, women dressed as quietly as possible. Every shool that had a black curtain for the Ark and a similar shaded cover for the reading desk hung them up in place of the red, blue or yellow curtain or cover. The real hesped was not to be delivered until the official memorial services were held but the Maggidim said sufficient to draw the tears from the eyes of their hearers and the woeful sighs from their hearts. The shools were crowded in anticipation of these references. No self-respecting maggid would allow the occasion to pass without paying the highest tribute to the great dead.

The event was, of course, the death of Queen Victoria and memorial services were held in synagogues throughout London at the termination of Shabbat 2nd February. The *Jewish Chronicle* of the previous day carried an announcement that a memorial service was to be held at Sandys Row Synagogue the next evening at 5.30 at which 'Rev. S. Melnick will deliver a discourse.' The following week the *Jewish World* reported that he had eulogised at the Plotzker Synagogue, while the *Jewish Chronicle* seems to have listened to him at Fieldgate Street. Neither mentioned Sandys Row.

At the end of July he preached at a service held at Kings Hall, Commercial Road at which a Sepher Torah for the Grand Order of Israel was consecrated. At the following supper an appeal was made to form a synagogue of their own and a Ladies Holy Vestment Society was formed. The next recorded event was of a more personal nature. On Monday 23rd December his eldest daughter Rosie married Abraham, eldest son of Samuel Hillman, at Princelet Street Synagogue, the officiants including the bride's father and the Chief Rabbi. Of this event, apart from a full set of official documentation, there appears to be no record. However, it is traditional that on the Sabbath prior to a marriage, the bridegroom, his father, the bride's father and possibly other relatives and guests are honoured by being called to the Torah reading at the bridegroom's usual synagogue. An account of this affair appeared, in Yiddish, in a book: *In My Days (Memoirs)*, published privately in December 1941 by Mr S. Oberman. (I understand that this book was written entirely from memory many years after the events described which may account for some of the

A Giant Among Giants 15

discrepancies and that an English translation of this book is in preparation.) In this account he informs us that Samuel Becker (sic) had two sons who were very learned in matters Jewish. The elder, Abraham, was to marry Shmuel Kalman's daughter and that on the Sabbath immediately prior to the nuptuals in accordance with this tradition, among the guests was the Chief Rabbi Dr Hermann Adler. The officers of the *steibel* in Black Lion Yard considered this an outstanding occasion; not only did they decorate the building itself but also that part of Great Garden Street which formed its approaches, the whole affair being described as 'a welcome fit for a king'. One must presume that Dr Adler addressed the assembly for the account only informs us that the bride's father conducted the service, his style reminding the writer of a *chazan* he had much admired whilst still in Poland.

Ten days after the wedding, Dayan Bernard Spiers died suddenly, after apparently recovering from an illness, the funeral being attended by Rabbi Melnick in his capacity as rabbi of the Chevra Tehillim of Princelet Street Synagogue. The inevitable memorial services were arranged, Shmuel Kalman being advertised as speaking at Spital Square Synagogue on 12th January at 3.30 p.m. and at the Plotzker Synagogue at 4 p.m. on the same day; the former eulogy only being subsequently reported.

On Sunday 2nd February the Chevra Bikur Cholim at 42 Lucas Street was presented with a new Sepher Torah at whose consecration Rabbi Melnick gave the address, he having conducted the services on the previous Friday night and Shabbat morning. This was followed by a *siyum* in the form of a supper at which he again delivered an address followed by the prayer for the Royal Family, the assembly finally dispersing at 2 a.m.

A Jewish dream throughout the centuries of dispersion has been the restoration of the Jewish state in the Promised Land. At this time a number of political organisations were working towards that end to such an extent that the dream was beginning to look remotely like a reality. The prime movement was that of Theodore Herzl which had captured the imagination of a significant proportion of European Jewry, but it was secular, rather than religious. Nevertheless it was gaining a strong foothold among the East End Jews; the established community was not interested in, indeed it was firmly opposed to, any nationalistic movement. Against this background a conference of presidents and *maggidim* of the various *chevroth* was called in late March 1903 'to consider what steps should be taken to strengthen Zionism in the synagogue and to inculcate the tenets of the Jewish religion in the minds of the young.' The meeting, led by Haham Dr Moses Gaster, took place at Kings Hall, Commercial

Road. A committee was set up to further these aims and included Rabbis Werner, Schneidman, Melnick, Regensberg, Rabinowitz, Chernofsky, Newman, Abrahamson, Simons, Heller and Dainow. Whether this committee ever met is a matter for speculation since no further reference to it is to be found. Another event of this time, which indeed might be said to have given impetus to the Zionist cause, was a pogrom at Kishineff when a mob of Cossacks attacked the Jews of that town, killing or injuring a large proportion of the community and doing much damage to property. Many protest meetings were held throughout much of the western world involving both the Jewish and general populations. In London most synagogues held such meetings and made collections to aid the victims. A memorial service at the Plotzker Synagogue and addressed by Rabbi Melnick raised £4 12s. 6d. and at the same event a raffle resulted in £14 being added to the building maintenance fund. On Tuesday of the same week a protest meeting was held at the Great Assembly Hall, Mile End Road which was 'attended by a large number of East End rabbis' although none of the reports mentioned any names.

During September Rabbi Melnick praised the work of the Chevrath Ezras Noshim when they presented the Lucas Street Synagogue with a Sepher Torah, its treasurer Mrs Tenser presenting a chased silver pointer, following which he conducted the service. During the same month he preached at the opening of the Bnei Brith Litobsky Synagogue, 156 Whitechapel Road. Subsequently he accompanied Dayan Hyamson and Rabbi Chaikin on an inspection of the pupils of the Commercial Road Talmud Torah. For the New Year festivals Rabbi Melnick preached at both the Great Alie Street and Plotzker Synagogues on the first day of Rosh Hashana, and again at the Plotzker on Yom Kippur. Another consecration attended was that of the new Bow Synagogue in Lincoln Street on 20th March 1905 followed by a dinner at the home of the treasurer Mr H. Chissick.

In this manner his public life continued, preaching at numerous synagogues, addressing meetings, conducting weddings, delivering eulogies at burials and tombstone consecrations, etc. One interesting meeting he attended and his first reported excursion away from the East End was at the Notting Hill Synagogue on 17th December to deliver a memorial address for the victims of the Russian atrocities. A collection, in association with the Sir George Jessel Lodge No 9 Order of Achei Brith and the Bayswater and Notting Hill Jewish Sick Benefit Society, realised £31 6s. 11d.

Towards the end of 1906 two innovations occurred; the first was that at the newly opened Beth Hamedrash and Reading Room in Mulberry Street

A Giant Among Giants 17

a series of winter Friday evening lectures was organised by the recently appointed Dayan Feldman at which, on 2nd November, Rabbi Melnick delivered a lecture in Yiddish entitled 'Historical review of the Talmud'. Like the others it started at 8 p.m. and was well attended. At a later date he gave a detailed history of Rabbi Shmuel Hanaggid (993-1055), secretary to King Habbus of Spain and holder of various other official offices. The other innovation was the introduction of Sabbath Afternoon Services for Working Men and Women at the East London Synagogue in Rectory Square during the winter months and which continued until the end of the first world war when they seem to have petered out. The address to these services was always in Yiddish and Shmuel Kalman was the most frequent speaker, giving the address almost every fortnight throughout the period. These were in addition to those at the Great Synagogue, Duke Street.

The death on Friday 3rd May 1907 of Dayan Sussman Cohen after a protracted illness came as a considerable blow to the community and the funeral at West Ham cemetery was attended by many leading figures including Rabbi Melnick. We have already seen that his preaching was not confined to the East End and it is on record that a number of congregations outside the confines of that 'ghetto' received the benefit of his erudition; thus on Shabbat Shuva (8th October) 1908 he gave the address at the barmitzvah of Philip, son of Mr and Mrs H. Blacker, at the West End Talmud Torah, Golden Square.

Poverty at this time was widespread and a sign of this was the annual distribution of boots at various institutions; at the Great Garden Street Talmud Torah, which he addressed, no fewer than 250 pairs were distributed. An event of 1909 was the seventieth birthday of Chief Rabbi Hermann Adler who received several congratulatory deputations, among them one on behalf of the Board of Shechita consisting of a number of *shochetim* and *shomerim* led by Rabbis Bronkhurst, Lipman, Melnick and First (of Edinburgh). At the end of the year he made a further excursion westward, this time to consecrate a new Sepher Torah at the fledgeling Bloomsbury Synagogue at 12 Chapel Street, Lambs Conduit Street when a number of related items and a Chanukah *menorah* were also presented. Soon after, the congregation obtained premises at 40 Lambs Conduit Street where it remained until its final demise in the early 1960s when the site was redeveloped.

In a different direction his youngest son Nathan possessed a fine voice and although not yet ten years old conducted the services at the Plotzker Synagogue on Friday night and Sabbath morning 4th and 5th February, a feat not all that uncommon at the time, nor was he the youngest ever to achieve it. Just over four years later he again did likewise, but more of this later.

To return to the Rabbi's westward excursions: the next was on 19th March when he preached, once again, at the Notting Hill Synagogue, this time at the Sabbath Afternoon service commencing at 3 o'clock; the question to be asked is, did he stay overnight or did he walk there? – a distance of several miles through the City of London, Holborn and the West End. Less likely that he stayed the night was the weekend of 13th-15th May when he preached at the newly opened Bloomsbury Synagogue in Lambs Conduit Street both on Shabbat morning and Sunday evening when a Siyum Hatorah took place. That same week saw the death of King Edward VII and he returned East to eulogise at both Sandys Row and Gun Street Synagogues on Sunday 22nd May. At the former, the *Jewish World* reported him as having 'delivered a stirring address to a crowded audience. Many were visibly moved when the lecturer compared the freedom enjoyed by those Jews who made England their home to the persecution they were subjected to under other rulers.' During June the *Chevra Chalukas Hashass* of the Scarborough Street Shool celebrated its first *siyum* on completion of study of the talmudic tractate Chullin, Rabbi Melnick giving a lecture on the tractate. During September he preached to the Reading congregation at a Sunday evening service.

With the start of 1911 he again spoke at the Friday night Jewish Institute meetings on the week's *sedrah* and at the end of January addressed a memorial service to Mrs A. Gaster at the Jewish Hospital Hall in Stepney Green. Two deaths of some consequence occurred this year, first that of Lord Swaythling, Samuel Montague, founder and President of the Federation of Synagogues in January, and then that of Chief Rabbi Hermann Adler during July. In memory of the former, Rabbi Melnick spoke at Princelet Street, for the latter at Sandys Row. (With this death an era in Anglo-Jewish history had come to an end for there was no obvious successor within the community and certainly no further Adler; Hermann's only son Alfred, who had entered the ministry, had died young.) Earlier that month he had addressed, once again, the Notting Hill Shool at the Shabbat afternoon service.

Among the Rabbi's friends was the *shammas* of the Great Garden Street Synagogue, Tobias Roth, an association which may well have gone back to the time of his first post in London. The association appears to have been a close one and on 11th July of this year he performed the marriage ceremony of Tobias's daughter Sarah to Adolph Michaelson, at her father's synagogue, this couple subsequently becoming wardens of the Jews Temporary Shelter. As we shall see shortly, this association became closer still.

Another westward excursion is recorded, this time on 28th August when, once again, he journeyed to Reading to address that community. Back in Spitalfields he joined Rabbi Werner in preaching at the presentation of a Sepher Torah to the Machzike Hadass Synagogue by Mr and Mrs A. Levy of Portsmouth at the end of September and at the end of the year he once again discussed the *sedrah Miketz* (Genesis XLI-XLIV 17) at the Jewish Institute, attending a *siyum* on tractate *Chullin* the next night, this time sponsored by the Etz Chaim Yeshiva at Dunk Street Sephardish Shool.

With the coming of 1912 the family once again upped home and moved, this time not in the local East End area, but to 25 Wayland Avenue, Dalston and a number of synagogues in that area received the benefit of his preaching. A major event of the year was the installation of Rabbi Mair Jung as Minister of the Federation at the Philpot Street Great Synagogue in June which he attended.

At the end of October his second daughter Ettie married David Weinbaum at the Wellington Road Synagogue, the celebrants being the bride's father, Dayan Hyamson and Rev. J. B. Levy. The ceremony was followed by a dinner at the Devonshire Hall, Hackney Road with the additional presence of Dayan Feldman and Rabbi Lazarus. One might conjecture that the move and the wedding were in some way connected. However, he remained there for some two years and when required to be in the East End over Friday night would stay with the Goldstein family of 78 Lower Chapman Street. At about the same time as the wedding a meeting of the *shochetim* and *shomerim* of both London and the Provinces was held to set up a trade union to be known as the Agudath Hashochetim and Shomerim, Rabbi Melnick being a member of the provisional committee. He remained a member of the committee until 1927 and for much of the time was a vice-president. In mid-December the West End Talmud Torah and Bikur Cholim Synagogue was presented with a Sepher Torah by its President Mr S. Wenter in memory of his late father; the service being conducted by Mr D. Brim, the reader, assisted by a choir of Talmud Torah boys and addressed by Rabbi Melnick. Also at the same service Mr P. Cornish presented a silver breast plate for the Scroll to mark his son's barmitzvah. The following weekend he spoke at the Institute on Friday night on the week's portion and at the Great Synagogue the next afternoon; a week later he was involved at the consecration of yet another new Scroll, this time at the new Bloomsbury Synagogue.

During 1913 Dr Joseph Herman Hertz was elected as the new Chief Rabbi. American educated, he had spent much of his ministry in South Africa but had recently returned west to take up a post in the USA and it was from there that he arrived on the RMS *Mauretania* at Liverpool on Tuesday 11th March. He was met at the dockside by representatives of the United Synagogue and other communities and travelled by train to London, to be met at Euston Station by further delegations including one from the Board of Shechita consisting of the Superintendent, Simon Myers; F.S. Cohen, President Agudath Hashochetim v'Shomerim; Revs. S. Bronkhurst and M. Schiff, Vice-presidents; Rabbis Hyman, Melnick and Rabbinowicz; Messrs Hirshbein, Hochman and Levinsky. Mr Myers read a message of loyalty on behalf of the delegation:

> 'It is my pleasure and privilege to introduce to you this deputation representing the Agudath Hashochetim and Shomerim of the United Kingdom and other officials engaged in the duties of Shechita. It is a source of satisfaction to us to be among the first in welcoming you on your arrival to the capital of the Empire and to have the early opportunity of assuring you that it will be our earnest endeavour to uphold and maintain under your wise jurisdiction a high level of efficiency, and by conscientious application to our duties and loyalty to your person to free you as far as lies in our power from every anxiety where questions of Kashrus are involved. I might mention that included in this delegation are gentlemen not only engaged in Shechita, but are able to exercise and do exercise Rabbinical functions among our brethren in that vast East End of London, with which you in your high and responsible office will shortly be closely acquainted.'

Despite living at Dalston the barmitzvah of his youngest son was celebrated at the Princelet Street Synagogue on 17th May (*sedrah Behar* Leviticus XXV-XXVI 2) where Nathan read the whole of the week's portion together with the *haphtorah* and conducted the entire Friday night and Sabbath morning services. After the High festivals young Nathan went to America to visit his two aunts in St. Louis, Minnesota where he conducted the service one Shabbat. The *New St. Louis Star* noted the event in its 31st October edition with a full length photograph of him dressed ready for service under the caption 'Nathan Melinek, 13 years old, youngest rabbi in the world who has arrived in St. Louis from London to conduct services at the synagogue.' The local Jewish paper, *The Jewish Voice*, appears to have ignored the event. In time for the same festival season Dayan Hyamson left London to take up a post with the Orach Chayim Congregation of New York and was presented prior to this with an illuminated album containing some 150 signatures of the *schochetim* and *shomerim* of London and Provinces. Speakers at the event were Mr Simon Myers, Rev. Bronkhurst, Rabbi Lipman, Mr F. S. Cohen, Rabbis Hyman, Melnick, M. J. Rabbinovitz, S. Rabbinovitz, Messrs. Trenner and Maizels. In December he lectured at the Beth Hamedrash and Jewish Institute on 'The Torah and Culture'.

During January 1914 he delivered a memorial to the late Mr L. Jablonski, Treasurer and Senior Warden of the Poplar Associate Synagogue, praising the deceased's work for the congregation and Hebrew classes in the presence of a large assemblage. About this time the family appears to have returned to the East End, taking up residence at 300 Commercial Road above the surgery of Dr Jeremiah Joseph Reidy.

With the outbreak of war in August the principal entries concerning Rabbi Melnick were in connection with collections in aid of Polish Jews who were having a particularly bad time with much of the fighting between the Germans and Russians taking place around them. Following the death in early 1915 of Lord Rothschild a memorial service was held at Princelet Street Synagogue at which he preached and the following January he spoke at the distribution of boots by the Malbish Arumim Society to poor and orphaned children who attended Brick Lane Talmud Torah; in April he again spoke at Poplar Associate Synagogue, this time at the presentation of a number of gifts. His summer holiday seems to have been spent with his son-in-law David Weinbaum, minister at West Hartlepool, where he conducted the Shabbat service. Subsequent to this Rev. Weinbaum appears to have resigned the position.

There next appeared in the *Jewish Chronicle* a series of unconnected announcements; I leave the reader to judge whether they can be strung together to make a whole. On 22nd March 1918 Mr A. Levy of Whitechapel Road, London and Landsdown Place, Hove thanked relatives and friends for letters and visits during the *shiva* for his late mother and also Rev. A. Levinson of the Brighton synagogue for his services and assistance during the week and Rev. A. Katz and Rabbi Melnick for their services. On 4th August at Brighton Synagogue Betty Steinberg was married to Ralph Cohen in a ceremony involving Rev. B. B. Leiberman of Brighton, Rev. S. Kahn of the New Dalston Synagogue and Rabbi Melnick. At the end of August there was a notice to the Jewish residents of Brighton and Hove that services during the ensuing High Holydays and Succoth would be held at the Portland Hall, Regency Mews, Regency Square, Brighton and these would be 'conducted by the well-known Rev. Samuel Colman Melnick (Shmuel Kalman). Services would also be held every Sabbath.'

Although there are no specific mentions of services to commemorate the armistice on 11th November a number were held, notably in the Great, Duke Street and Bevis Marks with many on various dates in other places. No doubt that he spoke at some of these, then Chanukah occurred at the end of November and there was the service of the Commercial Road Talmud Torah followed by entertainments to be addressed.

The Great War was scarcely over when the world was swept by a great influenza epidemic which, it is alleged, accounted for even more lives than the war itself. Among its victims was Shmuel Kalman's mother, Leah, on 14th January 1919, aged seventy-eight (not sixty-eight as stated on the death certificate) who was buried at Edmonton cemetery. A fee of two guineas was paid for the funeral since she was not a subscriber to the burial society.

The Friday night talks at the Jewish Institute in Mulberry Street were reinstated and he addressed the meeting on Friday 7th March, no record of his subject being found. The 31st August saw another milestone in East End history with the opening of the Jubilee Street Great Zionist Synagogue by Councillor H. Kosky. Dayan Chaikin addressed the congregation in English and Rabbi Melnick in Yiddish. One might consider it somewhat strange that, being opposed to the Zionist movement on religious grounds, he should have been involved in a religious community dedicated to its support. On Friday 12th December Rabbi Melnick again gave the address at the Jewish Institute, this time speaking on 'The Religions of the World and Judaism'.

1920 was to be an important year in his life for after twenty-four years he severed his connection with Princelet Street when, in time for Pesach, the new Great Synagogue at 262 Commercial Road, a converted Baptist Chapel, was opened with him as its Rabbi. The congregation had been formed some years earlier and had used the hall of the Philpot Street Synagogue until its own premises could be obtained. During May of the same year Rabbi Lipman retired as Rosh Hashochetim and was the recipient of a suitable presentation. The next event to record was the marriage of his third daughter Millie to Maurice, son of Tobias Roth, *shammas* of the Great Garden Street Synagogue at that synagogue on 16th June thus, as suggested earlier, bringing the association between the two much closer. The couple subsequently took up residence in Colvestone Crescent, Dalston. It was at this wedding that the bride's eldest brother Gershon met, entirely by chance, a cousin, May, of the groom, their engagement being announced only two months later. A lady of my acquaintance (a young girl at the time), and daughter of a former minister of the Bristol community, described to me the engagement party, for this was the first time she had seen the ceremony involving the breaking of a plate on such an occasion. Tobias's other daughter Esther had married a Samuel Roth (no relation) in April of the same year. His third son Raphael much later married Florrie, daughter of Rabbi Melnick's brother.

With a full time post as *shochet* and a large congregation to minister to, in addition to his advisory work with the Beth Din, there was little time left for other activities and rather fewer of these are reported so we now have to wait for further news of him until 10th December when he gave his annual address at the Jewish Institute on *'The Wars of the Hasmoneans'*.

At the end of January 1921 when, the *Jewish Guardian* of 2nd February reported, he took the chair at the annual meeting of the Agudath Hashochetim v'Shomerim, improved relations between the staff and the Board of Shechita were reported. However, it was considered still necessary for the members to be united and to be so more strongly than before since the improved position of the Board was due in no small measure to their own activities and there was now no opposition *shechita*. Once again he was elected a joint vice-president of the union, and in this capacity he preached the eulogy at the memorial service organised by the Agudath Hashochetim in July for Rabbi Nachum Lipman, the former Rosh Hashochetim. On 23rd August 1921 his eldest son Gershon married May Roth at Commercial Road Great Synagogue, a total of nine officiants being involved in the nuptials including the groom's father, all the *dayanim* and the minister of the Bristol community, the bride's home town. The Chief Rabbi was visiting the Commonwealth communities at the time!

As rabbi of the Commercial Road Great Synagogue, I was told, he conducted Friday night lessons during the winter months, starting at eight o'clock, discussing aspects of the week's portion. My informant recollected being taken there as a young boy by his father, one of his memories being of the sounds of gentle snoring from various quarters of the well-attended building; after an eighty-hour week this was quite understandable. In addition he gave a short lesson every morning at the end of the service to which many came who would not otherwise have attended a weekday service at all. But after two years there, another new synagogue opened, this time in Grove Street (now Golding Street) by the Chevra Bnei Poltusk and Makowa, which he was to serve until his sudden and untimely demise some five years later. No doubt these *shiurim* continued in the new post and he additionally is reported as speaking at various social occasions connected with the organisation.

At this last position his salary in his first year, according to the balance sheet, was £7 10s. 0d. plus two guineas extra for Pesach and 2s. 6d. for each of six weddings although this was not a full year. By his last year the salary had risen to £19 10s. 0d., the extra for Pesach remaining the same but with ten weddings although still at the same rate.

By now he was drastically reducing still further his activities. One reason, as reported in the *Jewish Guardian* of 12th December 1922, was that the Chief Rabbi had decided to improve standards of Kashrus supervision and to that end had convened a meeting involving himself, the Beth Din and the rabbis directly concerned, the scheme being funded by a grant from the Board of Shechita. Those present were five who were to supervise particular districts and three with more general fiats, Rabbi Melnick being one of the three. They were to exercise continuous supervision of the butcher shops and kindred institutions in their districts and to act generally as corresponding associates of the Beth Din in matters affecting the ritual needs of the particular localities in which their work lay. That is not to say that Melnick abandoned all other outside activities for he was still in demand to perform marriages, to address barmitzvahs and other occasions. One notable event at which he officiated was the setting of the tombstone to Mark Lazarus, sponsor of the No. 33 Lodge Order Shield of David on 29th April 1923 at Edmonton Federation Cemetery in which he referred to the deceased's active and lifelong communal work and benevolent spirit. Almost two months after this his second son David married Daisy Epstein at the New Synagogue, Stamford Hill. In September the same year he spoke at a memorial service to Mrs (or was it Mr?) Harris Tibber, a supporter of the South Hackney Talmud Torah at the Talmud Torah (or was it the Beth Hamedrash, St. Thomas' Road?) which was attended by many of the pupils and staff. Again in November he gave the address at one of the Friday night meetings at the Jewish Institute, this time on '*The struggle between Jacob and the Angel*'.

During 1924 he again moved, but this time only a few doors along the terrace to No. 314, above the surgery of Mr Maurice Batz, a dentist. Two notable memorial services took place that same year; although some two months apart they were geographically close: at the Jubilee Street Synagogue on 6th April 1924 when he preached the eulogy in memory of one of its trustees Nathan Bomberg and on 29th June at the Congregation of Jacob Synagogue just round the corner in Commercial Road in memory of Mrs R. Koenigsberg, in the course of which he is quoted as saying that as long as that synagogue existed it would stand as a testimony to Mrs Koenigsberg's untiring efforts on its behalf. (This is one of six synagogues still existing in the East End and a few years ago I had the privilege of assisting with its High Festival services.) Again at the end of November he lectured to the Jewish Institute, this time on '*Giving truth to Jacob and mercy to Abraham*'.

On 3rd March 1925 his youngest daughter Sarah married Sydney Wimbourne, Rabbi M. S. Rabinowitz and Dayan Lazarus assisting with the ceremony. The Great Garden Street Talmud Torah held its annual prize-giving in early June with Councillor Harry Kosky (President) in the chair and prizes distributed by Mrs Kosky; again Shmuel Kalman spoke, as usual in Yiddish, and appealed for more workers in aid of the institution. During the following summer his youngest son Nathan, who by now was taking up a number of communal appointments, married Annie, twin daughter of Rabbi M. S. Rabinowitz of Vine Court Shool and in October his annual address to the Jewish Institute was on the subject of '*acceptable words*'. The 1927 annual meeting of the union saw his retirement from activity and for the first time since its formation his name was not among its officers or committee. During June that year he gave the address at the reconsecration of the Congregation of Jacob Synagogue following renovation, a new Sepher Torah being presented at the ceremony. On 4th November he lectured for the last time at the Jewish Institute on '*Tidings of the Day*' and during mid-December spoke at the supper and ball of the Ladies Society of the Grove Street Great Synagogue held at the Grand Palais, Commercial Road. This, sadly, was to be his last reported activity for his sudden, untimely demise occurred only some six weeks later.

Note. Found in the synagogue files was a photograph showing a number of children who had survived the Kishineff massacre and were the first group on the way to Usishkins orphan institute in Palestine.

Chapter 3
The Death of Rabbi Melnick and his Legacy

Rabbi Simeon said, There are three crowns: the crown of learning, the crown of priesthood, and the crown of royalty; but the crown of a good name exceeds them all.
(Ethics of the Fathers IV, 17)

Although at some time it appears he was seriously ill enough to warrant the addition of the name 'Chaim', it must be assumed that this occurred in his younger days while still in Poland. There is no record that during his time in England did illness interfere with his normal work routine, although we must presume the regular round of coughs and colds did occur, but as he grew older signs of fatigue were beginning to show. After the 1927 annual meeting of the Agudath Hashochetim v'Shomerim he ceased to be an active member and on an occasion sometime in mid-1927 lost his balance while getting off a tram, falling against the side, so that he had to spend some time resting, rather suggesting that all was not well. Also he generally reduced his activity, spending more time at home.

It was on Thursday 26th January 1928 that he awoke feeling not too well. Nevertheless, Thursday being a busy day at the poultry yards, he carried on as usual. But it soon became evident that this was not just a matter of being a degree or two under, he was clearly seriously ill and his son-in-law David Weinbaum, also a *shochet*, was sent for to take him home, where he soon went to sleep on a couch. Attempts to wake him failed and a doctor was sent for who diagnosed a cerebral haemorrhage, ordering him immediately to the nearby London Hospital. Here examination indicated that the bleeding was due to high blood pressure although there was no obvious cause of the underlying problem. By this time he had lost consciousness despite which, a nurse reported, he was frequently seen trying to pull his *kupple* into its correct position. The family gathered around the bedside, and as the news spread, many leading members of the community came although few were allowed at the bedside. Sabbath morning services took on a mournful tone as prayers were said for his recovery in synagogues throughout the East End. Next day in many neighbouring Anglican and Catholic churches congregations offered prayers for a successful outcome but it was to no avail for he failed to regain consciousness and passed away at about seven o'clock that same evening.

Brief obituaries appeared next day in the Yiddish newspapers, *Die Zeit* describing him as one of the greatest interpreters of the Talmud seen in this country. On Tuesday a more detailed obituary appeared, together with a photograph, while the *Jewish Post and Express* carried an announcement above its title that an obituary was to be found on page 2. The obituaries spoke of the loss to the community in particular and to Judaism in general for he was frequently consulted from abroad on difficult problems; of his renown as an orator and scholar and of his career in England. Details of the funeral arrangements were also given: 'that the body would leave his home at 1 p.m. and proceed to the Grove Street Great Synagogue where the Chief Rabbi, Dayan Hillman and Rabbi Rabinowitz would deliver eulogies following which the cortege would proceed to the cemetery at Edmonton for interment.'

That accommodation for all who wished to attend the service in the tiny synagogue would be insufficient was accepted, especially since many prominent visitors had to be seated. What took place was entirely unforeseen. It was a mild February day, overcast but dry. People began arriving early outside the house, opposite the house, both sides along Commercial Road and into Grove Street on foot, in taxis, by tram, bus and underground. Soon all vantage points were taken with people on roofs and in windows, many perched precariously on structures not intended for that purpose while some women who fainted had to be treated in shops or doorways. Both foot and mounted police were called to control the crowds and make way for the traffic. As the coffin was brought out of the house to be put in the hearse the huge gathering surged forward, completely blocking the broad thoroughfare. Control of the crowd was lost and traffic was brought to a halt, the jams extending to Blackwall tunnel in one direction and beyond Gardiner's Corner in the other. Vehicles in neighbouring side streets were trapped, unable to proceed. Estimates of the crowd varied from 15,000 (*Jewish Post and Express*) to 20,000 (*Die*

Zeit); sadly police estimates are no longer extant. Commercial Road being a wide, main thoroughfare, little difficulty was experienced by the procession led by the hearse and followed by his three sons; brother; the Chief Rabbi; Dayan Hillman; Rabbis Gollop, Lev and Rabinowitz; the Sassova and Tritska Rebbes; several *chazanim*; the President, Mr J. M. Lissack, and other members of the Board of Shechita and most of the *shochetim* together with representatives of many synagogues and societies. Conspicuous by their absence, by all accounts, was any representative of the Federation of Synagogues. When however it turned into the narrow Grove Street, the road became totally jammed. The police had already cleared the parked cars but despite this the procession, even with its police escort, had great difficulty in passing along and several members of the foot procession, including the Chief Rabbi, were severely jostled. Immediately before the synagogue was St. Johns (Anglican) church whose bell tolled during these proceedings and displayed a notice 'We mourn with our Jewish friends', its minister being among the seated guests for the orations. On arrival police surrounded the hearse, enabling the coffin to be removed and taken into the synagogue where it was placed on a bier between reading desk and Ark. The scene there was indeed solemn and awe-inspiring, there not being a dry eye in the building. The sobbing became even more audible as Dr Hertz rose to deliver the first eulogy. He spoke in Yiddish of his previous appearances in this same Shool but, with great emotion, none so traumatic as this when tribute had to paid at 'the sudden passing of my great friend who loved his fellow man and who in turn loved him, to which the presence of tens of thousands this day testified. In spite of his great knowledge he had never lost touch with the ordinary man and was always ready to help in times of trouble and difficulty.' He quoted the talmudical adage: 'Happy is he who is great in Torah, who lives in Torah and dies with a good name; here was a man great in Torah, he was born in Torah, lived in Torah and died with a good name.' Dr Hertz spoke in the same terms as he had done only three weeks earlier at a memorial service to the late Chief Rabbi of Vienna Zvi Peretz Chayoth. Tribute was paid to the considerable assistance given to the Beth Din, to his predecessor Dr Adler and to himself. The deceased was a man of great knowledge, of humility and had achieved for himself the ultimate accolade of a good name. He was born into Torah, he lived in Torah and he died as he was born. The throng in the streets was testimony to his greatness in the way he went among the masses and was able to influence them. 'Happy is he who is great in Torah and labours in Torah and dies with a good name.'

The next speaker was Dayan Hillman who spoke of his prowess as a *shochet* and of how he had trained and encouraged newcomers to the profession, of his assistance to the Beth Din in many ways and his vast knowledge which was always available to the *dayanim*. Finally Rabbi Moshe Rabinowitz of Vine Court Synagogue also spoke of his great knowledge, the ease with which he was able to answer difficult questions and of his ability in conducting the synagogue services; they had lost a great and righteous friend and this day all Israel was mourning him. Chazan Halter intoned the memorial prayer prior to the coffin being returned to the hearse and the cortege reforming, again with considerable assistance from the police. Finally the sad procession left with difficulty, turning into Commercial Road, then New Road and Whitechapel Road, all deeply lined with ordinary people paying their last respects as the sad column wound its way to the Federation cemetery at Edmonton. As it proceeded others joined, the whole procession eventually consisting of some three hundred vehicles taking about twenty minutes to pass any given spot, police having to control all junctions on the way. Once again at the cemetery the gathering for the interment was so great that the gates had to be closed for safety reasons with hundreds outside unable to gain admission. Further eulogies were delivered by Rabbis Levene, Green, Gollop and Rabinowitz while Rev. Goldfine, appropriately enough of Princelet Street Synagogue, although in his capacity as minister of the Federation, conducted the service.

Graphic descriptions appeared in the Yiddish papers next day, a photograph of the scene in Commercial Road in some editions of the London evening paper *The Star* the same day; a brief obituary appeared in the *Daily Telegraph* next morning and in local papers that weekend. The *Jewish Graphic*, a weekly, devoted a full page to an obituary and description of the funeral scenes. Many paid tribute to the sympathetic behaviour of the police. The *Jewish Chronicle*, by contrast, carried a brief obituary written by Rabbi Gollop and the statement 'the funeral was largely attended'.

The subsequent *shiva* was attended by many leading figures from all areas of the community, and letters and telegrams received from many unable to attend. There remained one problem; as mentioned in the previous chapter Shmuel Kalman had two sisters in America and it was decided not to inform them until after the thirty-day period of lesser mourning so as to save them the full rigours of the *shiva* ritual. About mid-February a cable arrived from St. Louis saying that they had seen pictures of the funeral on a newsreel and asking why they had not been informed! (The death of Field Marshal Earl Haig, Commander-in-Chief of the British army during the 'war to end wars' had occurred the same night and journalists and cameramen were gathering in London for his funeral.)

A year later his tombstone with epitaph written by Dayan Hillman was consecrated. Once again there was an extremely large attendance; eulogies were preached by Dayan Hillman and others, the oration given by Rabbi Levene being published in Hebrew in his book *Diyuknei Shel Yaakov*. Translations of both this and the inscription appear at Appendices ii and iii.

Such was the wish of people to be buried next to him that by the end of the *shiva* when the family applied to reserve the neighbouring grave for his widow, it had already been booked and on her demise she was buried a considerable distance away in another block. She survived him by over nine years, dying on the second day of Succoth, 21st September 1937 in her seventy-sixth year from cardiac failure due to bronchitis and cerebral thrombosis.

The question must be asked; Why did so many turn out to pay their last respects? Other equally well-known immigrant rabbis such as Werner, Maccoby and Jung had died with large attendances at the funerals but nothing like this had been seen before in London, not even for a Chief Rabbi, and it is unlikely it will ever be seen again. Certainly he was the leading orator of his time, but Maccoby had a greater reputation and Jung had died suddenly in even more tragic circumstances; moreover both of these had held important posts with the Federation of Synagogues. It is difficult now, six decades later, to look back into that period and to understand the circumstances of the time, the poverty, the hope, the trust, perhaps the sense of community. All these, no doubt, played a part but there must have been something about the man himself that engendered so much sorrow at his passing. I can only speculate and repeat what others have told me and if the following appears to be looking through rose-tinted spectacles then it is because people tend to remember the positive and forget the negative things. He died before I was born and I, like several other of his grand-children, was named after him.

Probably he was of average height. In the street he was an impressive figure with flowing beard, dressed in long coat with silk hat and, except of course on Sabbath and festival, carrying a furled umbrella. He was a rather shy, private man, unlike many of his contemporaries, and did not advertise himself in their manner. He waited for the people to come to him for advice, counselling and help of many kinds, and come they did. Not for him the pickings of the comparatively wealthy, rather he identified with the poor immigrants, sharing their problems and lives, helping them when he could, frequently financially, often settling arguments and making peace between husband and wife and between other factions. Many stories are told about him of which I shall relate only a few.

All held him in great respect, Jew and Gentile alike, and not for him the need to hurry to the stop, for tram-drivers would stop for him wherever he was. Numbered among his friends was Inspector Eveson of Leman Street Police, himself a fluent Yiddish speaker (he probably spoke Yiddish better than my grandfather spoke English) and there were others whose names have long since been forgotten. Many an elderly man has told me that as a small boy when out shopping or whatever with his mother and on spotting the rabbi walking alone he would be told to walk with him for a few moments just to show respect, no need to say anything. Soon the youngster would be discussing his studies and as the conversation proceeded, so the little boys claimed, they learned more about Judaism in those brief minutes than in all the hours slogging away over *chumash* and *talmud*; in at least one case the boy became so engrossed that Mummy was lost and he had to be taken home by his new-found friend.

I was told of the young man fresh from Yeshiva appointed as rabbi of a congregation who was billeted with a lady whose strict and detailed observance of the dietary laws was disputed by no one. He would not eat meat nor any cooked food and, subsisting on a diet of raw vegetables and fruit, the effects soon began to show. The landlady became very worried and after much pleading with him to end his self-imposed penance, he eventually relented saying, 'If you will buy a new saucepan and get a chicken killed by Shmuel Kalman then I'll eat that.' Both kept their sides of the bargain and he recovered his old self.

Apart from being a general consultant to the Beth Din he carried out specific tasks for it. *Kashrus* supervision has always been difficult particularly in regard to *shechita*; one of his tasks was to make decisions on the suitability of meat and fowls after killing. At that time many women would buy live fowls for their Sabbath meal and take them to the slaughter yard to be killed, then home where they were plucked and opened. Others, even if they bought one already killed, would still insist on opening it themselves. If on doing so something questionable was found, the entire carcass was taken to the rabbi who would examine it and pronounce upon its fitness or otherwise. Thursday, especially in winter, was the busy day both for killing and for answering these questions. On one occasion (this story has come to me from several sources), a very poor lady came with her miserable chicken because its liver did not look right. Shmuel Kalman examined it very carefully, disappeared into another room for some while to refer to his numerous books on the subject, reappeared and took 1s. 6d. from his pocket, telling her to go and buy another. In her surprise she asked what the money was for. He replied, 'That's because I'm such an ignoramous that I can't make it kosher for you.'

Another function was to investigate the marital status of immigrant men applying for marriage in synagogues. It was the common practice for men to come from Eastern Europe to England, find work and accommodation, then send for wife and family as he himself had done. Occasionally it was used as an excuse to get away from the wife, find someone else and marry a second time. If this was suspected, Shmuel Kalman would be asked to investigate and contact the rabbi in the town from which the immigrant had come or even relatives already in this country. My father used to relate how on many occasions, the abandoned lady had been brought over by relatives and secreted in one room of their home while the erstwhile bridegroom was interviewed in another. After a while my father, or one of his brothers, would be told to produce the evidence and confront the runaway with his wife.

Another story, the accuracy for which I cannot vouch, concerned a meeting with a minister from the Reform movement. Part of the discussion (in Yiddish) went like this:

'Tell me, Rev. —, tell me what do the Reform people keep, do they keep Shabbos?'
'No!'
'Do they observe the festivals?'
'No!'
'Do they keep *kashrus*?'
'No!'
'Do they keep the laws of family purity?'
'No!'
'Well what do they keep?'
'They keep me!'

But perhaps it was in personal relationships that he was most admired. Comforting the mourners following bereavement was only a part of his brief, another was visiting the sick, yet these were routine activities; it was making peace between warring parties, settling family feuds and reconciling husband and wife where he really came into his own and earned the respect of the general public. A quick visit to them or they turning to him and a few well chosen words would break a deadlock or a situation which had long been simmering. Suitable words in a quiet corner comforted the bereaved especially after a particularly tragic death. In sad times, in times of trouble as well as on joyous occasions, he was with the people. He never forgot his own humble beginnings in the tiny town in Poland where he was born and grew up. No part of any rabbinic dynasty, his father was a tailor, his mother and grandmother just scraping a living in the local market followinq the death of husband and father at the early age of thirty-five and well before her marriage. He had lived in the grinding poverty of that time and place. Nor, for that matter, did any of his sons become *rabbanim*. Even here in England circumstances were such that community funds at times were insufficient to pay the rabbi his weekly wages and he was not alone in suffering from this problem.

But it was as a preacher that he came into his own for there were few equals and sermons of up to four hours duration were not uncommon, delving deeply into some *halachic* matter without the benefit of notes or other mnemonic, perhaps using only a few books to read accurately quotations, although even this was frequently unnecessary. Crowds gathered to hear his words of comfort and cheer. The hardships of daily living and working, the slum houses and sweatshops were forgotten for those few brief hours, spellbound by his erudition and oratory. Attention was undivided for fear of missing some important point on which the entire argument might hang. Often the crowds were such that space within the building was insufficient to accommodate all who wished to hear and they would gather around windows and doorways like a school of Hillels to drink the words of wisdom being preached. At times even the Great Synagogue in Dukes Place had insufficient accommodation when he spoke there and police had to be called to keep the excessive crowds from overwhelming the building. Sadly, little record of those orations remains for even were there tape recorders available most of these were given on Sabbath and Festival when such instrumentation is not permitted. These speeches were always in Yiddish, usually not prepared in detail beforehand and newspaper reporters seemed unable to cope with the material. In any case they would have had to rely on memory for writing on the holy days is forbidden. Any notes he may have made have not survived, nor does a book of thoughts on the Talmud which he appears to have written; the only written material available consists of a few marginal notes in his copy of the Talmud and other books which have come into my possession. There is evidence that he completed the writing of the book around the year 1914 and then submitted it to some of the great talmudic authorities in Poland for their criticisms. Unfortunately it got caught up in the war and appears to have been irretrievably lost. No copy seems to have come to light in England. I am told that after his annual Shabbat afternoon address at the Great Synagogue he would speak to the children from which a particular item stuck in the memory of one of his listeners. He was discussing the passage (Genesis XLVIII) in which Joseph brings forward his two sons Manasseh and Ephraim to be blessed by Jacob on his death bed who on seeing them asks, 'Who are these?' Why did Jacob not recognise them? for he knew them well having lived there for seventeen years. Shmuel Kalman said that usually when Jacob saw them they had been wearing their normal house clothes but on this occasion they had been summoned hurriedly from the University which they were attending, still wearing academic dress which made them seem like strangers to the grandfather.

On one question he seems to have been somewhat schizophrenic. As a traditional, observant Jew he was passionately in favour of a return to the Holy land but at the same time he was equally passionately opposed to the prevailing and dominant but non-religious Hertzlian movement. As such he felt he could not join its ranks even though many of his colleagues were strong supporters. Instead he allied himself with the Haham, Dr Gaster, Rabbi Werner and others in an attempt to set up a religious Zionist organisation in which basic religious ideas were given equal prominence to the nationalistic ones. Nevertheless, as we read in the previous chapter, he took part in the opening ceremony of the Jubilee Street Great Zionist Synagogue whose membership was strongly aligned to the Hertzlian movement.

Shemura matzos, those used at the *seder* service on the first two nights of Pesach, were not bought but personally made by himself. He would go with his sons to Bonn's factory in Assam Street where the special flour was available and hand mould and bake the items. On the intermediate Festival days he did not lay *tephillin* and observed the three fast days following them. Although very strict himself on observance of the religious *minutiae* he recognised that not all were up to his standard and that living conditions militated against some of these; thus he would not allow the *chazan* to use a tuning fork on Sabbath or Festival but refused to answer women who asked if they might wheel the baby in the pram on Shabbat; on certain details of the Pesach laws he was again somewhat more lenient than most. He was more interested in the spirit than the dead letter of the law nor did he try to set up alternative organisations as so many of his contemporaries and those after him did. To him the dictum was that 'the custom of the community was sacrosanct' so that changes without the consent of the community were untenable. Nor was he prepared to look over his shoulder to find out what others might think before making a decision, indeed it was very much a case of the reverse where others looked to him first. One of the major problems in this area was *shechita* and several attempts to set up rival organisations for that purpose were thwarted by his own intervention, often after bitter arguments. On matters of *shechita* he bent over backward to give permission for the fowl to be used and, especially when financial hardship was involved he might even pay for the replacement himself.

Being himself an immigrant, thus with first hand knowledge of conditions in Eastern Europe, he could neither agree with nor understand Dr Adler's almost total opposition to the wave of immigration nor to his insistence that English alone should be spoken by them. Although living conditions in London's East End were far from ideal, they were often better than those experienced in Poland and Russia. Further, they were not subject to pogroms and other deliberate campaigns of hate. It was not until news of the Kishineff pogrom reached his ears that the Chief Rabbi really appreciated the state of affairs in those parts. By this time it was too late, with moves afoot to restrict the influx with the support of much of the original, settled community. Another dislike of his was the Jews' Free School in Bell Lane which he regarded with almost as much hostility as the various missionary groups active in the district.

Perhaps some idea of the respect in which he was held is shown by the Kelly's Post Office Guide where he is described as 'Great Rabbi': no one else have I seen so described in Britain. (In France the term 'Grand Rabbin' is common.) All who knew him revered him long after his passing and many who were too young at the time or even not yet born tell how their parents remembered and spoke of him. Rev. Saul Levy of the New Synagogue, at the barmitzvah of one of my brothers, quipped that he lived with the Almighty since his final years were spent at 314 Commercial Road; the Hebrew letters for 314, slightly rearranged, make up one of the names of G-d. At the funeral of my father, his eldest son, Rabbi Maurice Landy of Cricklewood Synagogue, briefly recalled those times describing him as 'A giant among giants'.

Chapter 4

History of the Princes Street Synagogue to 1893

Unless the L-rd build the house, they labour in vain, they who build it.
(Psalm CXXVII)

The tendency for population movement out of the immediate confines of the City of London was given added impetus by the Great Fire of 1666. On the eastern side the important route north out of Bishopsgate through Norton Folgate and Shoreditch was well-developed. In the late seventeenth and early eighteenth centuries the Artillery ground on the East of Bishopsgate-without was built over and this development spread into the Spittle Fields immediately to the east. During July 1708 Messrs. Wood and Mitchell started acquiring land in that part known as Joyce's Garden. A decade later Samuel Worral built two houses on the easternmost extremity of the estate, known as 18 and 19 Princes Street. Three years after, in February 1821, Worral took out a mortgage on 18 Princes Street and the house immediately to the rear, 30 Browns Lane (now Hanbury Street), to secure a loan of £300. At the end of the following year both houses were sold to John Nevill, citizen and needlemaker of London, for £270. The freehold of 18 Princes Street remained with his descendants for 277 years until sold to the Federation of Synagogues who, in turn, sold it to the Spitalfields Historic Building Trust in 1980. The house at the rear, now 30 Hanbury Street, had been sold separately by 1823.

The earliest tenants were part of an important Huguenot refugee family named Ogier, a daughter of which, Louisa Perina (1729-1807), married a Samuel Courtauld, and after his death at a comparatively early age, returned in part to the traditional family silk trade, at the same time continu-

A Giant Among Giants

ing her husband's trade as a silversmith. Her second son George lived for a while in the USA but his son, Samuel (Samuel Courtauld III) returned to England, set up in business as a throwster at Bocking in Essex and thus founded the Courtauld Company of today. It is not certain that Louisa's particular branch of the family actually lived in this house. She was living in Spital Square at the time of her marriage and was buried in the crypt of Spitalfields Church. However, it is known that she had a brother Pierre or Peter and an Ogier of that name, probably an uncle, is recorded as the tenant until past 1740. He is believed to have raised a troop of twenty-eight of his employees to resist the advance of the young pretender.

The house was used for spinning and weaving silk, a typical trade in the area at that time. It is possible that they added a workshop at the rear to supplement the space in the garret. This, however, is another story not within my remit. Restrictions on the import of foreign silk cloth were removed in 1826 and the silk trade in Spitalfields collapsed. From about this time a drastic change in the use of the building took place. It next appears to have been occupied by Alfred Lavey, a professor of music, until 1847, who was followed by Lewis Abrahams, a wholesale pickle and sauce manufacturer from 1851 to 1857; Mrs Mary Ellen Hawkins used it together with the two adjoining houses, as an industrial school, an apparently short-lived venture for in 1859 Isaiah Woodcock, a carver and gilder, held the premises until 1864 when he was succeeded by George Flint, an engineer, for a further five years. The next tenant was the Loyal United Friends Synagogue whose story, as far as it can be ascertained, occupies the remainder of this book.

The Loyal United Friends Friendly Society (Hebrew name חברת נדבת חן) was founded in 1862 by a group of immigrant Polish Jews led by Jacob Davidson, Coleman Angel and Harris Levy (usually known as 'Mr Harris'). The objects of the Society were to provide financial relief when needed and free medical treatment, including hospitalisation if necessary, during illness. Burial and tombstone would be provided on the death of the member and his wife and a grant provided during the week of *shiva*, all for a small weekly fee. In addition, although not a primary object of the society, it was decided to organise religious services as there was no synagogue in the area at the time. Initially these services were held in rooms in Fashion Street but membership was growing and by 1865 the Rosh Hashana and Yom Kippur services took place in the Sussex Hall, Leadenhall Street, such was the pressure on the space. For the following two years the same hall is known to have been used and in 1869 they were held in the Zetland Hall, 51 Mansell Street, Rev. Aaron Barnett from

Adelaide, Australia conducting the services. Of this period this is all that is currently known, and there is evidence that the minute book for the period prior to 1874 had been lost by 1907, the time of the demise of the Society.

The tenancy of the house with a workshop in its garden at 18 Princes Street became available when George Flint vacated the premises during 1869 and thus attracted the attention of the society's officers. This was felt to be ideal for converting into a synagogue and a twenty-year lease on the building was obtained from John Sparrow Bawtree or Henry Bawtree who was looking for a tenant prepared to take a long term lease. With their permission the garden was excavated to provide a basement level general meeting hall in addition to the ground level prayer hall. Ladies were to be accommodated in a first floor gallery around three sides. Support for the gallery was by a row of slender cast iron columns with a spiral groove adornment set on beams in the ceiling of the basement below, in turn supported by plain columns. The new synagogue was approximately 16 ft. by 40 ft., with the rear ground floor room forming an integral part of the prayer hall, the overall design being based on that of the New Synagogue in Great St. Helens. Folding doors were fitted so that the front room of the house could be used for additional seating for the men and the first floor back room for the ladies when necessary. The Ark was at the far (north) end in a gated apse, the roof above painted azure with gold stars; the *bimah* was situated centrally, seating on either side of it facing sideways, that behind forward. Natural light was provided by a skylight and stained glass windows at the far end, artificial light by means of gas lamps and two sun burners. The two original basement rooms were converted into separate meat and milk kitchens serving the hall, first floor front room used as the office and two top floors for living accommodation for synagogue staff or let out to paying tenants. The architect was Mr Hudson, the builder Mr Langmead. Cost of the conversion was £1,100 paid for, in part, by the membership and the remaining £500 by means of a public appeal.

Consecration of the new synagogue took place during the afternoon of Sunday 4th September 1870. The synagogue was filled to capacity with the congregation in Holyday attire, some, including the Honorary Officers, wearing additional decorations. Rabbi Bernard Spiers pronounced in Hebrew, 'Open unto me the gates of righteousness that I may enter and praise the L-rd'. The doors opened and the procession led by the Rabbi and carrying Torah Scrolls entered to the strains of *Boruch Habo* (Blessed is he who comes in the name of the L-rd) sung by the choir. Seven circuits were made as Psalms XXX, XLII, XLIII, CXXII, C and XXIV were chanted by Rev. Barnett and choir. The Vice-President Isaac Shuter handed the key of the Ark to the President, Jacob Davidson, who opened the doors and placed the Scrolls inside. Rev. Barnett then read the afternoon service after which Rabbi Spiers made the dedication address in English:

> We could exclaim with the Psalmist, this is the day which the L-rd has appointed, we will be glad and rejoice therein. It is a bright day, a joyful assembly is this, an hour of joy and thanksgiving for our Heavenly Father has preserved us alive, sustained us and brought us to enjoy this season, and we have been permitted to consecrate this place of worship. We need not describe here the conditions, the place, the exertions and the objects of this society: they are sufficiently known to most of you. Looking at this beautiful little synagogue we ought to give thanks to our Heavenly Father for having deigned to enable the wardens to erect this house. We will not dilate on the time, trouble and money they have expended. But some of you might be asked if it were necessary to have a synagogue attached to your society, seeing that there are already so many places of worship in this metropolis. You can give a plain affirmative answer. This place of worship was necessary in this part of the city, it is intended for the working classes who are hindered by distance from frequenting the larger synagogues. A small synagogue is for a sincere worshipper equal in every respect to a larger one, as the Almighty has been pleased to declare to us through Moses our teacher: 'In whatever place I record My Name, I will come unto thee and bless thee.' In order to duly consider these questions Psalm LXXXI tells us 'How dearly beloved are Thy dwellings O Eternal of Hosts! My soul longeth, yea, even fainteth for the courts of the Eternal: my heart and my flesh shout to the living G-d:' also 'Happy are they that dwell in Thy house, they shall continually praise Thee, Selah.' From these texts we learn first to resort to the house of G-d to say our prayers; secondly to pray with devotion and, thirdly to pray often. First we resort to the house of G-d. When David was banished from Jerusalem on the occasion of his son Absalom rebelling against him, and in consequence could not visit the Sanctuary nor abide in the Tabernacle, what fervent prayer did pour forth that he might be permitted to seek the L-rd again in His House? 'One thing I have asked of the Eternal that I will seek after; that I may abide in the House of the Eternal all the days of my life to behold the pleasantness of the Eternal and to enquire in His Temple.' Why then had David such an earnest desire for the House of G-d? Because he wished to enquire there. For this reason we, likewise, should have a desire to resort to the House of G-d; in this place 'my soul longeth', in the number of the faithful people to utter praises to His Holy Name in the place where the word of G-d is read and expounded. Yes, my brethren, frequently resort to the House of G-d. Rely upon it, faith has such a heavenly influence that a blessing will continually proceed from His Holy place, and will enter our hearts when we enter into the House of G-d. We may deprive ourselves of an earthly

pleasure, but worship will be a light and a guide to us in our earthly pilgrimage. In support of my argument I will quote an allegory from the Midrash Rabba: 'There was once a king who had an only daughter. A prince solicited her hand, married her and wanted to depart and take his wife with him. The king addressed him thus. "My daughter whom I have given thee, is my only child; part with her I cannot. But where you go to dwell provide a room where I can live near you as I cannot leave my daughter."' In like manner the Holy One, blessed be He, said I have given you a Law, it is My Law, do not forsake it, where it is I must be; therefore in order not to be separated from you I command you that you shall make Me a sanctuary that I may dwell among you. Delight in the sanctuary and let us dwell in it. How dearly beloved are Thy dwellings. Secondly we should pray with devotion. If we go to synagogue our prayers should not be the mere voice of our lips without earnestness of purpose. Our sages say of thoughtless prayer; 'Prayer without devotion is like a body without a soul.' Prayers must be said with devotion, my heart and my flesh, not merely the moving of the lips. Yes, let us pray as our sages teach us. Prayer directed to G-d with humility is heard. Let us lift up our eyes to Heaven with earnestness and sincerity. Thirdly and lastly, we should pray often: Happy is he who dwells in Your House; these are the concluding words of our text. Do not entertain the opinion of those who enter the house seldom; who direct from dark earthly thoughts think to be able to perceive bright visions without fervour of devotion, even as the hinges of a door become rusty when seldom opened, even so the heart grows cold when we do not often stand and appear before the L-rd. We frequently look upon our attendance at synagogue as a wearisome occupation and are only too glad to dispense with it. Here in this plain and unpretending House of Prayer – here, where there is nothing of a too imposing character to distract our attention – we can pour out our griefs, bear our trials and confess the wound of our hearts through the voice of prayer. You should come often to this place of worship. You who are oppressed by care and by the sore diseases of the heart, come often and do not wait for a particular festival or holyday when you may think it a special duty to appear before the L-rd. We ought, rather, to esteem it as an inestimable privilege to be permitted to pray to the Almighty. Our prayers do not benefit G-d, they do us good. Prayer is much greater, say our sages, than the offering of sacrifices. Happy are they who dwell in Thy house, they shall be continually praising Thee, selah. Let us follow the lessons of our text, let us come often to synagogue, let us pray often when we are happy or unhappy, joyful or sad; let us pray with gladness and reverence, serve the L-rd in reverence and rejoice in its witness. You members of the society have incurred considerable expense in rearing this Mikdash Me'at. Do not profane it with idle gossip but enter it with brotherly love and an united heart free from all unholy thoughts.

He concluded by invoking a blessing on the building, adding a prayer for the Queen, the Chief Rabbi and also for peace and the coming year. The

Rev. Barnett then read the prayer for the Queen and Royal Family. This was followed by a complete list of donations to the building fund and by chanting of the dedication ode composed by Chief Rabbi Dr Herschel by the Reader accompanied by the choir. The service terminated with Oleinu and the choir singing Psalm CL.

The appeal for the outstanding sum was launched following the opening, appearing in only two successive issues of the *Jewish Chronicle* and, unusually for its time, no lists of donors were issued. The wording of these two appeals is of some interest.

Prince's Street Synagogue Spitalfields.
The committee of management of this place of worship earnestly APPEAL to their brethren for ASSISTANCE in building the synagogue which was consecrated on 4th instant. The expense of the building amounts to about £1,100 of which a balance of £500 is still due. A synagogue was badly needed in the neighbourhood. The committee trust their pious brethren will aid them liberally in this emergency. Donations will be thankfully received by Mr. J. Davidson, president, 15, Princes-street, Spitalfields.

The second notice was couched in the same terms but the name of L. Isenberg, Esq., corner of Lime Street and Leadenhall Street, was given as an additional recipient of donations. Both these notices announced, in addition, speakers for the next day: Rabbi Spiers at 2 p.m. on 10th September and Rev. M. Berliner, Headmaster of the Borough Jewish Schools, at 10 o'clock the following Sabbath.

For the High Holydays Rabbi H. Harris delivered a sermon of which the *Jewish Chronicle* promised an abstract the next week; alas, it never appeared! Other advertised speakers in this early period included Mr Meisels, chief secretary to the Chief Rabbi, Rev. S. Singer and Rev. B. Ascher. However, Rabbi Spiers was the most frequent, usually at the afternoon services. The membership stood at one hundred and twenty and the synagogue was frequently full with only standing room left. On the intermediate Sabbath of Pesach 1871 (5631) Rabbi Spiers addressed the congregation when he discussed the exodus from Egypt. Other sermons were delivered by 'a Polish gentleman' on the first day, another on the seventh day and by the Rev. N. Guinsberg on the last day. Rabbi Spiers spoke again on the second day of Shavuot and on 24th June. In this latter sermon he discussed the revolt in the wilderness led by Korach and concluded by a reference to the recent death from smallpox of Numa Edward Hartog, a young communal worker and senior wrangler at Cambridge University only two years earlier.

Tragedy was to strike the President at the end of July for on the 30th his wife Caroline died aged only forty-one giving birth to a stillborn son. Otherwise, it appears, there was only one daughter of the marriage. It seems that Mrs Davidson had been an active partner to her husband in the formation of the Loyal United Friends Friendly Society and the synagogue. At a general meeting of the Society held on 8th August with Isaac Shuter in the chair, a letter of condolence on behalf of the Society was handed to Mr Davidson, copies entered in the minute book and published in the *Jewish Chronicle* of 11th August. The preacher at the afternoon service of the previous Sabbath, 5th August, was Rabbi H. L. Harris who, the *Jewish Chronicle* reported, took his text from Ethics of the Fathers Chapter III: 'Akabya, son of Mahalalel said; Reflect upon three things and thou wilt not come within the power of sin: know whence thou camest, and whither thou art going, and before whom thou wilt in future have to give account and reckoning.' Discussing the text he referred to the death of Mrs Davidson, urging his listeners 'not to indulge in too much grief when the Almighty in His infinite wisdom sees fit to afflict us with pain, poverty and bereavement but to look to our own deeds and not to defer until tomorrow, works that can be done today.'

At this period the religious functionaries, rabbis, ministers, readers, *shochetim*, etc. had all been born abroad and received all or part of their education outside Britain. Consequently, considerable interest was shown when the services at Princes Street during the first weekend of December were conducted by Marcus Haines at the invitation of the President and Wardens. Mr Haines, English born, a former pupil of the Jews Free School in Bell Lane, and student of the recently formed Jews College read the services in 'a most inspiring and efficient manner'. (During July 1874 Haines was elected minister/first reader of the Western Synagogue.)

At the end of the year the Prince of Wales was taken ill, prayers for his recovery being recited during the ultimate Shabbat of the year. The same report also noted that Rev. Barnett was 'about to relinquish his position as reader, we hope for a more lucrative one.'

His immediate successor was Barnett Ginzberg, although the Post Office Guide consistently spelt his name as Giuzberg and listed him as minister until 1875 even though he had left before Pesach 1873. The High Holyday services of 1872 were conducted by Rev. Ginzberg assisted, gratuitously, by Mr M. Barnett of West Ham. The traditional celebrations of Simchat Torah were marked by Woolf Cohen and P. Prince entertaining the members in the vestry room with the president in the chair. Toasts were drunk to the *Chasanim*, the clergy and the 'readers', Messrs Cohen,

Price, Landeshut and Barnett replying. At this celebration, the former Vice-president Isaac Shuter was presented with a gold chain and watch, suitably inscribed, in recognition of his services.

Four successive issues of the *Jewish Chronicle* beginning with that of 14th February 1873 contained advertisements for a Reader at a salary of £50 per annum. The same issue containing the first advertisement also informed us that on the previous Sabbath Moses Lewis Cohen of Zakroczym, Poland had conducted the services as a candidate for office and had made a very good impression on the members. No word was given of any other candidates and we only read of Rev. Cohen having commenced duties as Reader in time for Pesach. The same report also raised the question of including the smaller synagogues within the communal union (i.e. the United Synagogue). The wardens for the year, Joseph Warschawsky and H. Ehrenberg, were formally installed on the Shabbat after Pesach when Rev. Cohen demonstrated that he was possessed of more than a fine voice by delivering a discourse on 'Unity and Harmony', an essential prerequisite for enabling the congregation to continue in as prosperous a manner as it had done previously, he suggested. Shavuot coincided with the barmitzvah of Jonas, son of the former named warden, who, to celebrate the event, presented tablets for either side of the Ark containing the Prayer for the Royal family 'written in an ornamental style in Hebrew and English, forming a welcome addition to the appurtenances'. The next recorded presentation took place on Shemini Atzeret when Mr Robinson of Bell Lane donated an Ark curtain in thanksgiving for the recovery of his child from a serious illness. Guest speakers prior to this event included Rabbi B. H. Ascher who spoke in aid of the Metropolitan Hospital Sunday Fund in June when £11 3s. 0d. was raised, Mr Meisels who preached on the Shabbat before New Year and Rabbi Spiers who delivered a sermon on the afternoon of the second day of that festival.

With the festivals over a meeting of considerable significance took place, yet went unreported in the press of the time. The occasion was the evening of 19th October corresponding to Tishri 29th 5634, the assembly being convened by Harris Levy for the purpose of founding a society for reading and studying the Psalms and carrying out such charitable acts as visiting and supporting the sick and the bereaved, of burying the dead, of marking the graves and giving such assistance to the dependents as might be necessary. All members would be involved in these activities but a rabbi would be employed. The organisation was named 'The Society for Chanting Psalms and Visiting the Sick' (חברה תהלים ומשמורים); it was the first of its kind in England although similar societies have been recorded elsewhere from the beginning of the fourteenth century. The new society rapidly became a major force within the synagogue environment and was copied by many new congregations as they were set up or soon after. Membership was restricted to persons of the Jewish faith who need not have been synagogue members. (A rule book was published in 1893, presumably to coincide with the reopening of the synagogue that year.) Its formation quickly made its mark on the friendly society which changed its rules subsequently to include provision for a rabbi and *minyan* men for *shiva* costing up to 14 shillings. The two organisations do not appear to have become rivals and frequently co-operated together as and when the opportunity arose.

By 1874 Mr Ehrenberg decided that the time for a change at the top had come and was replaced by 'Mr Harris' who, in league with his brother Woolf and Messrs. Greenzweig and Gutmacher presented a new *Torah* Scroll, the usual ceremony taking place on Sunday 24th May followed by a dinner in the hall. For some reason Joseph Adler was not invited to this celebration and the first minute book still extant records that he took umbrage at the omission, threatening to resign all offices and also his membership. At this affair two further Scrolls and a mantle were promised. The first of these Scrolls materialised almost immediately, for the *Jewish Chronicle* reported only three weeks later:

> One of the most flourishing of the so-called minor synagogues which exist in the East End of London is the Prince's-street Synagogue, situate in Prince's-street, Spitalfields. This synagogue – like all other synagogues in the neighbourhood of Spitalfields and Whitechapel – is in connection with a chevra or friendly society, the objects of which chiefly assume a religious character such as providing Minyan during the week of mourning of a member, etc. The society with which the neat little synagogue in Prince's-street is connected is styled חן נדבת חברת and is in a prosperous state, the numbers of its members – who are almost entirely foreigners – increasing so rapidly that mention is already made of a desire to enlarge the present synagogue.
>
> In this synagogue on Sunday was held a ceremony peculiar to the 'minor' synagogues – at least a similar ceremony has not taken place in any of the principal synagogues within living memory – and it consisted of the consecration of a Sepher Torah presented to the synagogue by a member of the chevra, Mr. W. Cohen. The service, which occupied three hours, closely resembled that held at the consecration of a synagogue. The Scrolls of the Law were taken to the doors of the synagogue, the usual excerpts from the Psalm were recited after which the seven circuits were made by the officials and others carrying Sephers, the Psalms recited being those

chanted at the consecration of a synagogue. The service was ably conducted by the Rev. Mr. Cohen, the Reader (who has a very pleasing voice) assisted by a competent choir. After the Scrolls had been placed in the Ark, Rabbi Spiers delivered a sermon in German. In a lengthy discourse he admonished the congregation not to leave the Torah in the Ark but to take it out and study it whenever possible. In illustration he told the story of a young man leaving home to further his studies. His father presented him with a large book and begged him to study it and bring it back on his return. The son promised to do so but found the book too bulky to carry around from place to place and so secreted it at home among his other belongings. While away he won many prizes and gained degrees at several universities. On his return several years later his father congratulated him on his successes and asked if he had read the book. The young man assured his father he had done so and produced the tome. His father thumbed through and suddenly producing a £5 note said 'No, my son, you did not take the book with you for if you had you would have found the treasure I put inside before I gave it to you.' The preacher went on to ask how many did likewise with the holy Torah given to them by their Heavenly Father; they put it by, it was burdensome, they think it is of little use. They do not even read it and so fail to see and avail themselves of the treasures contained in it. He begged them to study it, to teach it to their children to cause them to become familiar with it and with the Hebrew language much neglected in the age. The sermon was concluded with a prayer and the service ended with the prayers for the Royal Family and the donor, and a long list of donations in honour of the occasion was read. This was followed by a supper in the basement vestry room over which Mr Jacob Davidson presided. In proposing the 'Health of the Queen and Royal Family' he reminded the company which consisted of about one hundred members and visitors, of the freedom they enjoyed in England, how grateful they should be and that they should be foremost in testifying that gratitude by love and loyalty for the Sovereign and institutions of the country. The toast was drunk with marked enthusiasm. Further toasts comprised 'the clergy', prosperity to the chevra, the wardens, the treasurer and committee, the vice-president, the press, Mr. Shuter, the chairman and finally the visitors.

The High Festival services that year were conducted by Rev. Cohen again assisted, gratuitously, by Mr M. Barnett of West Ham; Rabbi Spiers delivered the traditional talmudical discourse on Shabbat Shuva. Other events of the year included the presentation of matching Ark curtain and mantles by Messrs. Newman Levy and Jacoby and a board to record the names of donors.

At the start of 1875 a separate meter was presented for the gas supply to the *Ner tamid* and the synagogue and house gas supplies were separated.

With the average working week being eighty hours and Sabbath morning services commencing around half past eight, many preferred to spend the morning in bed always assuming they were not actually working, and attend the afternoon service instead. This fact of life was reflected in many of the major synagogues as well as the smaller ones such as Princes Street. Here a leading preacher would deliver a sermon, usually in Yiddish, at the end of the afternoon service beginning at about 1.00 or 1.30 and a substantial attendance could be guaranteed. Indeed, even the Great Synagogue in Dukes Place might often have standing room only for latecomers and occasionally even this might not be available. During the year the Jewish Association for the Diffusion of Religious Knowledge decided to promote a monthly speaker at Princes Street and these included Revs. Marcus Haines, Dr Hermann Adler (later Chief Rabbi), A. L. Green, I. Harris, and I. Meisels. Princes Street remained a major venue for meetings of the Association for many years.

The traditional talmudical discourse on Shabbat Shuva was announced in advance to be given by the Maggid of Slutsk, Rabbi Hirsch Dainow, known as the 'Russian Maggid' with service commencing at 4 p.m. Long before the appointed hour every seat and all the standing room were taken and still more arrived. The front room and gallery were made available but soon the throng spilled onto the pavement outside. In an attempt to reduce the crowd, an announcement was made that the learned gentleman was indisposed and would not attend. The idea backfired and a near riot ensued, the police having to intervene to cool matters.

Probably the most regular of speakers here and in other East End synagogues was Rabbi Spiers who gave his services gratuitously, walking to the district from his home in Gower Street, Bloomsbury and delivering sometimes two sermons on the same day. To show their appreciation, a meeting of members under the chairmanship of Mr Abraham Berg, a warden, was held on 23rd November which decided to invite the neighbouring synagogues to join in raising a testimonial for the valuable services he had rendered. On the following Friday notices of the appeal appeared in both the *Jewish Chronicle* and *Jewish World*. On the final Sunday of the year the Russian Maggid again came to Princes Street, this time to address the 'Maggid Society' set up to retain his services in London. (That the society managed to keep him in London was without doubt, but their efforts were not entirely successful for he lived in abject poverty and died of pleurisy on 6th March 1877 at the early age of forty-five leaving a wife and several children.) This time there were no riots.

The collection realised £120 and on 19th April 1876 Rabbi Spiers was presented with a purse of gold and a suitably inscribed coffee service at a meeting at Princes Street with the contributing synagogues represented.

A Giant Among Giants 47

On the Tuesday prior to this presentation the annual meeting of the synagogue had taken place, somewhat later in the year than usual, at which it appears a resolution was moved and lost that the reader's salary be increased from £60 to £100 per annum. The following Friday an advertisement appeared in the *Jewish World* from Rev. Cohen, thanking those who had given the motion their support. A week later an announcement appeared in both that paper and the Jewish *Chronicle*:

> Princes Street Synagogue The Excutive [sic] of the above Synagogue do hereby contradict the statements made in an advertisement which appeared in last week's *Jewish World* respecting the salary of the reader and notify the following: Wanted a חזן and בעל קורא for the above synagogue. Salary £60 per annum. Applications by letter only to be made to A. Heiser, secretary, 17 Bell Lane, Spitalfields.

During the course of the ensuing week the row was patched up and Rev. Cohen reinstated, appropriate notices appearing in both papers. To complete the picture of those few weeks Rabbi Spiers delivered a sermon before the Musaph service on 1st April. (In July Rabbi Spiers was elected a Dayan of the London Beth Din, being the only candidate.) Repairs to the roof and other parts of the building were effected by a Mr Falkenstein, presumably the Vice-President, at a cost of £33 10s. 0d.

The High Holyday services were conducted by Rev. Cohen assisted as in previous years by Mr Barnett and 'several religious discourses were delivered in the peculiar jargon favoured by the Polish section of the community'. Shortly after, on 28th October, a new preacher appeared in the form of Rabbi Joseph Kohn-Zedek who spoke in German on the portion of the week and was well received.

During this year two meetings took place although there is no evidence that either achieved its stated purpose. Both had the object of setting up Talmud Torah classes for children to attend after school; the first in January, chaired by Mr A. L. Freedman and supported by Rev. Cohen; the second in October addressed by Rev. A. L. Green among others.

One of the peculiarities of the three organisations constituting the Princes Street Synagogue was that all officials, both paid and honorary, were elected on an annual basis and, as we shall see later, this persisted at least until 1952 if not throughout the life of the congregation An advertisement appeared in the *Jewish Chronicle* of 13th April 1877 that Rev. M. L. Cohen would read the services at the newly opened East London Synagogue during the coming week as a candidate for office. During this same week the annual meeting of the Princes Street Synagogue took place at which Rev. Cohen failed to be elected, possibly of his own volition. He also failed to be elected at the East London. Whatever the reason, the position was advertised the following Friday with applicants required by 8th May. Emanuel Spiro of Birmingham read the services on the following Shabbat. The first of the candidates appears to have been Israel Michael Michalowski of Paris, the advertisement adding that admission would be by ticket only (obtainable from the secretary) and members were requested not to bring children with them. Subsequent candidates were Moses Lewis of Cardiff, Herman Davids of Breslau and A. H. Eisenberg of Warsaw. At the invitation of the Chevra Tehillim, Dayan Spiers addressed the congregation on the second day of Shavuot, taking as his text Psalm LVIII v.8. On 9th June Rabbi Joseph Messing of Witkova, Posen, Poland delivered the sermon.

At the end of September Mr Hollander the Vice-president presented a wedding canopy consisting of square wooden uprights set into the floor with iron hook separators at the top (still in existence) as supports for the fabric cover. At the behest of the United Synagogue marriages under its own auspices but at reduced rates were being solemnised at Princes Street from the previous month and lasted through until late 1890. The next chapter discusses the background and some of the events of this period. The 5th November issue of the *Jewish Chronicle* carried an advertisement for a חזן and בעל קורא at £100 per annum.

In January 1878 tragedy struck one of the wardens, Mark Cohen, when on the 11th his twenty-month-old son Isaac died, followed two days later by his wife Pauline aged thirty-five. A vacancy for a reader which had been notified the previous September was filled by Alexander Tertis of West Hartlepool who was inducted into office on Friday evening 1st March. Later that month, following the annual general meeting, the members adjourned to Camperdown House for a dinner at which both Jacob Davidson and Joseph Gerstman were presented with sets of Festival Prayer books in recognition of their services to the congregation. During April a chapel in Whites Row with seating for seven hundred came up for auction. It was decided to attempt to buy it but it went for £4,300 with Davidson able to bid only £3,500.

Perhaps the only event of 1879 worth recording was only indirectly related to the synagogue, although the meeting took place on its premises. The Society for the Relief of Jewish Poor Emigrants had recently been established to assist newly arrived immigrants from Poland to find employment, learn a trade and become self-sufficient. Under its president Coleman Angel, it had been formed by a group of employers to assist recent arrivals who did not yet qualify for support from the Board of Guardians, and who, to avoid starvation, had gone to the missionaries for assistance. (The Board of Guardians did not give assistance to immigrants until they had been in the country for at least six months.) Although this meeting was poorly attended, the society had nearly two hundred members, many of them employers, and more were being sought. A second public meeting was to be held a month later.

The year 1880 opened with a peculiar incident; the reader and *shammas* hired the Garrick Theatre in Leman Street to put on some kind of entertainment to which 'A Member' took exception and wrote a rather facetious letter to the *Jewish World* detailing how the officers should follow on and link the Synagogue to the theatre environment. This was followed by a letter from the president in which he stated that the gentlemen concerned had hired the theatre in their private capacities and the synagogue as such had no connection with the affair; he suspected that the letter had come from one of a defeated minority during some dissention. A more important event of the year was the death at the end of March of one of the regular preachers. Rabbi Messing had been rabbi in Gastein and Schempin in Germany before coming to England and had written six volumes of commentaries on the Bible and Talmud as well as various manuscripts on cabalistic and other subjects. He spoke regularly, alternating between the Princes Street and Kalischer Synagogues and was greatly beloved by a large circle of Polish and German admirers. On Sunday 18th April Princes Street Synagogue held a memorial service at which Rabbis Joseph Kohn-Zedek and Nachum Lipman preached, the latter also referring to the recent death of the Russian Maggid, Rabbi Hirsch Dainow mourning the passing of 'two such eloquent preachers who had done much to raise the moral condition of the foreign Jews'.

The second day of Shavout is by tradition the anniversary of the death of David, King of Israel and writer of the Biblical Psalms. The *Chevra Tehillim* on this day marked the occasion by reading the entire book and subsequently adjourning to the vestry hall where traditional fare was served but not before speeches by the president Henry Harris on the advantages of the society and by Rabbi Lipman. Although no further reports of such a celebration have appeared, the account books rather indicated that this was an annual event.

Apart from a number of visiting speakers and readers there seems little to report during 1881 until 22nd October when Abraham Smith, a warden, presented a new Ark curtain with matching cover for the reading desk and two weeks later Rabbi Louis Cohen of Berlin delivered the sermon while

Rev. Woolf Sparger of Vienna conducted the service, Mr Sparger repeating the exercise on the two following Sabbaths owing to the illness of Rev. Tertis. Rabbi Cohen was subsequently elected Rabbi of the Chevra Tehillim, thus becoming its first permanent Rabbi, frequently delivering sermons at the Sabbath afternoon services in the synagogue. At some time he was also elected rabbi of the newly formed Mile End New Town synagogue, both positions being retained until his demise some fifteen years later. (There is no evidence that that synagogue ever appointed a successor.)

In February 1882 Jacob Smith, brother of the warden, presented a Sepher Torah, the usual ceremony being performed. At the end of the month a collection on behalf of the persecuted Jews in Russia realised £22 and for the High Festivals Rev. Tertis was assisted by Mr S. Goldberg.

The next important event in the life of the congregation did not take place until the end of the next year when a meeting of members took place to decide how to mark the centenary of Sir Moses Montefiore, this being a major event not only in the Anglo-Jewish community but also in much of Britain and the British Empire. The meeting, which was also attended by representatives of various East London Foresters Courts (a friendly society grouping), decided to go along with a suggestion by Mr J. Brill, Editor of *Lebanon* to supply the colony of Pesach Tikvah in Palestine with two pumping stations to be named 'Ba'aroth Moshe' so as to relieve the water shortage there. A committee with Jacob Davidson as its chairman was formed to further the matter.

Prior to the formal celebrations, Rev. M. M. Alexanda (generally known as Moshe Michal) conducted the services on Shabbat 22nd March 1884 and at the end of April a presentation in the form of a set of Sepher Torah bells and pointer together with a tablet with the Ten Commandments was made to Jacob Davidson by Abraham Heiser on behalf of the congregation. In making the presentation he proposed the health of the President who, in turn, proposed the health of the other officers; Lewis Gold, Joseph Rosenthal, Joseph Gerstman, Charles Posener and Woolf Cohen, each, in their turn, replying. They were followed by Rev. Barnett. Another guest preacher, this time on Saturday 12th July, was Rabbi J. Bernstein of Littan Courland. The official service marking Sir Moses Montefiore's hundredth birthday was arranged for Sunday 26th October, to be conducted by Rev. Tertis with Rabbi A. Hirschowitz as the preacher. That this event may have seemed at one time in doubt was due to the peace of the building having been rudely shattered at about 8 p.m. on the previous Tuesday when an accumulation of gas exploded causing a fire, shattering some glass and damaging fittings. The fire was quickly extinguished with the aid of a few buckets of water, the overall damage not being serious enough to cause any postponement of the special service. In his sermon Rabbi Hirschowitz spoke of Sir Moses' philanthropy and self-sacrifice in undertaking his many long and dangerous journeys in order to relieve his persecuted and suffering co-religionists.

Another event of the year was the publication of the book of rules of the Loyal United Friends Benefit Society, the name-change presumably being at the behest of the Registrar General of Friendly Societies with whom it was registered as No. 4335 in February 1885.

Apart from the marriage affair described in Chapter 5 the only events of the years 1885 and 1886 worth recording were an attempt to buy the house next door, No. 17 (now 21), which might have prevented a riot some eighteen years later, for £1,200; and visiting readers Revs. N.L. Sapirstein on 2nd May and Hyman Jospe of Strasbourg, 30th January and 6th February.

A Special General Meeting was called for 16th February 1886 to discuss a recent affair in which a former member had been voted £15 for his defence in a court case. The secretary had declared it illegal and Mr Davidson paid the money himself with Lewis Gold and Woolf Cohen offering a bill which was subsequently dishonoured. The two were sued with Gold alleging that Davidson had £200 of the Society's money. A vote of confidence in the president was carried. It was stated that the money had been paid into court and the meeting ended in uproar. At a further meeting on the 25th recriminations continued; Davidson dropped all charges against Cohen whilst Gold was fined 5s. for his misconduct then and 21s. for misconduct at the previous meeting and asked to resign his synagogue membership. The general meeting at the end of June elected Jacob Davidson as Synagogue President for life.

The year 1887, by contrast, started with disaster and went on to festivity culminating in a major event in Anglo-Jewish history. A Jewish theatre club had been set up at the rear of No. 3 Princes Street (now No. 6) by Jacob Adler (no relation to the family of the Chief Rabbi), a well known Yiddish actor, much to the chagrin of the establishment. On Tuesday evening 18th January 1887 during a performance of *The Gypsy*, a popular light opera of the period, at about 11 p.m. there was a call of 'fire'. A stampede for the single exit door ensued and, to complicate matters, someone with safety in mind turned off the gas supply so that all the lights went out. The entire audience of nearly 600 was left to grope its way out in the darkness, some having got out then returning to try to find relatives.

In the ensuing mayhem many fell and were trampled on; twelve women, four boys and one man died and many more were injured and had to be treated in hospital. On the following Shabbat Rabbi Cohen preached a special sermon and offered up a prayer thanking the Almighty for His mercy in sparing so many of the children from a fearful death and, indeed, that the disaster was no worse. Rev. Tertis recited the memorial prayer for the dead. (It is interesting to note that this particular disaster prompted much of our current safety legislation for theatres and similar institutions.)

With the advent of the annual meeting Rev. Tertis decided to resign from his position as reader in order to concentrate on his other communal activities. The vacancy having been advertised, it was announced that the Pesach services would be conducted by Oscher Rubinstein of Suwalki assisted by his two sons, aged eleven and thirteen, who had received awards in Chicago and New York for reading services. Unfortunately Mr Rubinstein was indisposed at the beginning of the festival and only conducted services on the last two days and the subsequent Sabbath. For the next eight weeks candidates for the position conducted services, members being 'respectively requested to attend all these services in order to observe the capabilities of the various candidates'. Two major services were held on 18th June, both conducted by Rev. B. Ginsburg and Rabbi Cohen and both well attended. The morning service was devoted to the annual appeal on behalf of the Metropolitan Hospitals Sunday Fund as a result of which £5 was donated to the charity. The afternoon service was given over to a celebration of the golden jubilee of Queen Victoria. This latter event was celebrated a second time by a supper at Richmond House, Spital Square attended by some one hundred members and guests. With the meal over and grace having been said, Jacob Davidson, the President, rose to propose the health of Her Majesty and in so doing referred to the hospitality extended to foreigners by the country. The toast was received with much cheering and drunk with great enthusiasm. The Vice-president then proposed the health of the President, noting that this year also marked the silver jubilee of the Loyal United Friends Benefit Society of which Mr Davidson had been President for all that time having rendered invaluable services, regardless of the circumstances. Accordingly he was presenting Mr Davidson with a handsomely framed and beautifully illuminated address the text of which read:

This testimonial was presented to J. Davidson, Esq., Ab 17th 5647, Sunday August 7th 1887 by the Committee and Members in recognition of the valuable and zealous services rendered by him for the last 25 years as President of the above Synagogue, an office which he still holds with the greatest ability and to their entire satisfaction, and they hereby place on record their grateful and cordial appreciation of his untiring efforts in promoting the general welfare of this Society to the greatest advantage of the congregation.

In replying Davidson said that this was the fifth occasion on which he had received a testimonial. During some comments on the affairs of the synagogue he said he hoped shortly to be able to announce a scheme for the abolition of offerings during the reading of the Torah which, he hoped, would be accepted by the membership. In time for the High Festivals Moses Claff was appointed Reader.

On 16th October a meeting took place at the Spital Square Synagogue as a consequence of some correspondence between its President Mr H. Berliner and Samuel Montague MP and, no doubt others, with the object of 'forming a federation of minor synagogues and *chevroth* in the Spitalfields and Whitechapel areas now that the influx of refugees from the officially inspired pogroms following the assassination of Czar Alexander II had caused the formation of numerous such institutions', many in unsafe or unsuitable buildings. There was considerable interest in the project, about fifty representatives from seventeen congregations attending, Princes Street being represented by its President. The Chairman of the meeting, Samuel Montague, reviewed the situation and the case for federation. After some discussion the resolution to form a federation was carried and it was decided to invite a representative of every *chevra* and minor synagogue in East London to a preliminary meeting at Spital Square Synagogue on Sunday 6th November at three o'clock to discuss plans for the federation. That some of the *chevroth* invited to the meeting were not represented is obvious from a notice in the *Jewish Chronicle* the previous Friday to the effect that several invitations had been returned in the post marked 'not known'. In fact only eighteen such institutions were represented at this second meeting which formally gave birth to the Federation of Minor Synagogues, the word minor being dropped about two years later. At this meeting Davidson asked whether it was intended to propose a distinguished leader of the community as President; as, unless this were done, or the chairman (Samuel Montague) himself consented to become acting President, the Federation would fail for want of efficient organisation. The Chairman replied that he would endeavour to obtain the services of Lord Rothschild or his brother Leopold de Rothschild as President and that he himself would be pleased to act as Vice-president.

The first formal meeting of the 'Federation' took place on Sunday 2nd December at the Jewish Working Men's Club in Great Alie Street; Princes Street being represented by Coleman Angel and Isaac Rosenthal.

The next important event in the history of the community does not appear to have occurred until March 1889, when on the 16th the sermon was preached by Michael Adler, a graduate of London University and student at Jews College. This was a case of 'Local boy makes good' for he had grown up in this very synagogue; his father, a cousin of Chief Rabbi Nathan Adler, served on the committee and was sometimes a warden; and his mother later became President of the Ladies Holy Vestment Society. He himself had celebrated his barmitzvah there some nine years earlier and went on to become minister first of the Hammersmith and then the Central Synagogues. Among other appointments he held was the Senior Jewish Chaplaincy to the forces in which he saw active service on the Western front during the first world war and received the DSO.

In June yet another Torah Scroll was presented, this time by Abraham Smith of Great Prescott Street and Michael Adler addressed the congregation a second time on 24th August in which he discussed the significance of the month of Ellul.

The initial twenty-year lease by the Loyal United Friends Friendly Society was now approaching expiry. On 29th September, the position was secured when Henry Bawtree of 72 London Road, Clapton, Middlesex, a descendent by marriage of John Nevill, granted a fifty-year lease of the premises at an annual ground rent of £55 to Jacob Davidson of 15/16 Princes Street, Spitalfields, boot manufacturer; Joseph Gerstman of 19 Church Street, Spitalfields, tailor; and Coleman Angel of 116 Commercial Street, Spitalfields, warehouseman, as lessees. The property is described simply as the 'messuage tenement or dwelling house situate and being on the north side of and numbered 18 Princes Street in the county of Middlesex and also the yard and workshop in the rear thereof'. A plan of the 'workshop' drawn in the margin appears to be identical with the synagogue although there is no reference to this fact in the document. The only reference to the use of the premises was a prohibition to carry on the trade of a 'tanner, skinner, currier, fellmonger, leatherdresser, blacksmith, brightsmith, coppersmith, wheelwright, cooper, farrier, butcher, slaughterman, tallow melter or chandler, soapboiler, plumber, brazier, glazier, brewer, beerhousekeeper, victualler or any or either the said trades or business or any dangerous, noisy, noisome or offensive trade or business whatsoever'. Also, unless agreed otherwise, the tenants would cause the premises to be restored to their former condition as a private dwelling house at least three months before the expiration of the term. It is somewhat difficult to square these prohibitions with the use of the building for the manufacture of pickles and sauces for nearly a decade from 1850, nor am I prepared to speculate as to whether the initiative for this move came from Henry Bawtree or the synagogue management. At any rate, with the future now assured, the synagogue applied to the June meeting of the Federation at the same time as the Old Castle Street synagogue for a loan to allow reconstruction of the building. The application was passed to the executive committee which in July the following year deferred the applications with the consent of the Presidents.

Chief Rabbi Nathan Adler, who had been ill for some time and many of whose duties had been taken over by his son Hermann, died on 21st January 1890. Two weeks later, on 2nd February a memorial service was held at Princes Street attended by two of his sons, Marcus and Elkan, Hermann officiating that day at the laying of the foundation stone of the Hammersmith Synagogue. The service was conducted by Rev. Claff with sermons preached by Rabbis Louis Cohen and Chaim Zundel Maccoby, the Kamenitzer Maggid; 'the latter, by his style of delivery, bringing tears to the eyes of many of the crowded congregation.' The 25th July issue of the *Jewish Chronicle* carried a peculiar notice, the background to which I have been unable to trace:

> I, Abraham Goldman of 58 Brick Lane herewith apologise to Jacob Davidson Esq. President of the Princes Street Synagogue for the offensive observations uttered by me in a moment of haste and which I sincerely regret.

It is possible that this was one of a number of rowdy meetings since during the previous April another member of the committee had been fined one guinea and required to write an apology to the president. For the remainder of the year little of significance happened worth recording other than the matter of the cheap marriages being transferred to the East London Synagogue as described in the next chapter.

There was an unusual event on Sunday 2nd March 1891. A ceremony took place at the New Dalston Synagogue at which not one but two Scrolls of the Torah were completed, one destined for that synagogue, the other for Princes Street, the congregation consisting of members of both. The donors were Mr and Mrs Solomon Freedman and the final letters were written by Dr Adler, acting Chief Rabbi, Rabbi Lerner, Rabbi of the Federation and Mr Shipper, *Sopher* of the Beth Din. Following the Afternoon Service Dr Adler addressed the assembly on the importance of the study of the Bible taking as his text Joshua I v.8: 'This book of the Law shall not depart out of your mouth; but thou shalt meditate therein day and night, that thou mayest observe to do all that is written therein.' He was followed by Rabbi Lerner who observed that the Ark of the Covenant was encased without and lined within with pure gold. That this was a symbol of what our own hearts should be when the word of G-d found a resting place there, our inner self should be as unalloyed gold. Guest preachers during the year included Rabbis Lipman and Lerner and on 18th July Rabbi I. A. Alexander from Dorbain, Government of Kowno (Poland). The year ended on a sad note for on 2nd November Rebeccah Deborah, wife of Rabbi Cohen, died, apparently childless, in her sixtieth year.

The election during 1892 of Hermann Adler as Chief Rabbi came as no surprise since he had been delegate Chief Rabbi during his father's later years, had been acting Chief Rabbi during the interregnum and was the only candidate under consideration. As was usual, the new incumbent toured the various congregations under his jurisdiction and on the morning of 12th March addressed the Princes Street Synagogue, the occasion being Shabbat Zachor. All seats were taken and there was little standing room left. He spoke mostly in German of the way anti-semitism had manifested itself in Jewish history, taking Amalek as his example, and of the duty of the community in preventing its appearance in this country. While they should not deviate from the ways of their faith they were obliged to 'adopt the humanising manners and refining customs of the land of their adoption which so hospitably welcomed the hunted refugee.' Hebrew was the language of Divine Revelation and, therefore, the language of our prayers; all other tongues were of equal sanctity as the vehicle of communication between people. It was important that the immigrants learned the English language to enable them to earn a living and become regarded as equals by their fellow countrymen. In so saying, he drew attention to the various classes where English was taught.

For the New Year Rev. Tertis, despite having resigned as reader, returned to assist with the services. He had never entirely broken his connections with the organisation and, indeed, still lived in Princes Street. On the first day of New Year Rabbi Lerner spoke about the significance of the Shofar. But the pressing problem was the state of the house especially after the survey by the architect to the Federation. The refurbishment of the building was estimated to cost some £600 and of this only £200 could be raised from its own resources, or rather those of the Loyal United Friends Friendly Society. At least £400 was required and a new approach to the parent body was essential. This request was more successful than the previous one and, as we shall see, resulted in major changes to the building.

Chapter 5
Cheap Marriages

He who is mighty above all, He who is blessed above all, He who is great above all, may He bless the bridegroom and the bride.
(Marriage service)

The communal scene had been dominated by the four city synagogues which for all practical purposes controlled all religious and charitable institutions as well as the Board of Deputies of British Jews. The Rabbi of the Great Synagogue was considered the religious authority of the Ashkenaz community and it was not until 1846 that the provincial congregations were given a say in the selection process on the death of Rabbi Hirschell. It was his successor Dr Nathan Marcus Adler who was formally titled Chief Rabbi. Under Act of Parliament the Board of Deputies appointed marriage secretaries to synagogues and this meant that, apart from the Bevis Marks Synagogue, marriage solemnisations were controlled by the other three city congregations. As far as possible the Chief Rabbi himself officiated at all wedding ceremonies.

In 1870 the United Synagogue was founded by union of the Great, Hambro, New, Central and Bayswater Synagogues representing over a thousand members, many of them amongst the wealthiest Jews in the country. In effect it retained control (and still does) of almost all the major communal institutions. Left out of the union were the Western, Maiden Lane, Borough (which soon joined) and a number of small synagogues (including Princes Street) in the Aldgate and Spitalfields areas catering in the main for a much less wealthy sector, largely recent immigrants from Eastern Europe. It was not until the late 1890s that marriage secretaries were appointed to the members of the Federation.

Among the problems presented by these new arrivals were an inability to speak English and an even lesser knowledge of English law and customs particularly in regard to marriage and divorce. In Jewish law a man marries by placing a ring on the right index finger of the bride in the presence of two witnesses who must be observant Jews and making the declaration in Hebrew, 'Behold you are consecrated to me, by token of this ring, according to the law of Moses and Israel,' the marriage contract is given to the bride or her representative, the seven marriage blessings are recited and the couple are considered married, no other formality being required. However, both English law and the Chief Rabbi required further documentation. Both demanded prior notice and evidence that both parties were free to marry; the Chief Rabbi, additionally, wanted evidence of the Jewish ancestry of both parties and that no other impediment in Jewish law existed. What in fact was happening was that a significant number of couples, unable to afford the minimum three guinea fee (this representing four to five weeks' wages or even more for a working man) stipulated by the United Synagogue, or through ignorance of the correct procedures, or both, would gather the required quorum with a willing rabbi in a convenient room and have the ceremony performed there. They were known as *'Stille Chasenes'* (many of these took place in the basement hall of Princes Street Synagogue) and having no legal basis in English law raised many problems if and when the marriage broke up. Also, any children of the marriage would be illegitimate. An alternative was to go to a registry office and have no religious ceremony.

In order to overcome the problem and in response to much agitation not least from officialdom, Mr Goldhill moved a motion at the March 1877 meeting of the United Synagogue council that the Executive examine the marriage regulations in order to allow persons who could not afford the standard fee to be married in synagogue. The motion was vigorously opposed by Lionel Cohen, a vice-president, but was passed by the meeting. The executive set up a sub-committee to study the entire problem of marriage fees and procedures and produced a series of recommendations which were put to the meeting of 15th June by Lionel Cohen and adopted after a full discussion. They were:

1. That the ordinary marriage rate for marriages celebrated at any of the Constituent Synagogues remain at £3 3s. 0d., as at present (inclusive of Dr. Adler's fee). The existing extra charge of £2 in cases of marriages not solemnised in the Synagogue to be maintained without alteration.

2. That persons desiring to be married at a lower rate than the above shall be entitled to 'claim' the right of being married for the sum of 10s. 6d.
3. That marriages celebrated under the conditions of Clause 2 be solemnised at one of the so-called minor Synagogues.
4. That in the case of the marriage of seatholders of any of the Constituent Synagogues, or any of their children, or of persons who may at any time have been contributing seatholders for any period amounting in the whole to two years, or any of their children, a power of reduction or remission of the larger fee (specified in Clause 1) be vested in any two of the honorary officers of that Synagogue, the marriage to take place in the Synagogue of which the bridegroom is or becomes a member in the same manner as if the fees had not been reduced or remitted. Every application for such reduction or remission to be made on a form of application provided for the purpose and to be submitted by the local secretary to his Honorary Officers for decision.
5. That a similar power of remission of the smaller fee (specified in Clause 2) be vested in the Overseers of the United Synagogue, with respect to marriages solemnised in one of the minor Synagogues, the marriage to take place there in the same manner as if the fee had not been remitted. Every application for such remittance to be made on a form of application to be provided for the purpose and to be addressed to the Secretary of the United Synagogue, who shall submit it to the Overseers for their decision.
6. That the Rev. the Chief Rabbi be not called upon to solemnise marriages celebrated under terms of Clauses 2, 3, and 5.
7. That the marriages celebrated at one of the minor synagogues under Clauses 2, 3, and 5 be solemnised by such one of the accredited Ministers of the Constituent Synagogues, and registered by such one of its secretaries, or in such rotation, as the Executive Committee may from time to time determine.
8. That the amount of the wedding charges be received as at present by the Constituent Synagogue, in connection with which the marriage is celebrated.
9. That full publicity be given in such a manner as the Executive Committee may, from time to time deem advisable, to the regulations under which marriages may in future be solemnised at various rates, and to the possible consequences resulting from irregular marriages.
10. That all marriages not solemnised at the private residences of either of the persons married, or in rooms provided by them, be solemnised without distinction whatever in the synagogue, unless prevented by the actual performance therein of Divine Service, or by the synagogue being under repair, or by the marriage having been inadvertently registered for the Synagogue Chambers.

(Marriages of US members (or their children) who had been allowed reduced fees were held in the vestry or other room and not in the Synagogue itself.)

The Princes Street Synagogue was recommended as the most suitable and its president, following discussion with the United Synagogue officials, agreed to allow such marriages to take place without fee. In August detailed regulations for such marriages were published, a choice of Cutler Street, Prescott Street, Princes Street, Sandys Row and Scarborough Street Synagogues being available. Ceremonies were to be performed by the ministers of the three city synagogues and the newly established East London, acting in rotation. Although there was no challenge to the principle of the low cost marriages objections were voiced to the absence of the Chief Rabbi and that they were to be held in the 'minor' synagogues. Many felt that to exclude the poor from the main synagogues was 'to add insult to injury', one member going so far as to suggest that if a 'hole-in-the-wall synagogue' had to be chosen then the United had one of its own at the Hambro. This feeling was echoed in the Jewish press of the time which also objected to the exclusion of the Chief Rabbi from these ceremonies. In fact about a hundred members of the city synagogues formally protested while the Hambro raised a motion at the next council meeting that all these should be held on its premises but owing to the lack of time it was put back to the next meeting where it was withdrawn. Rabbi Joseph Kohn Zedek was deputed to bring these new regulations to the notice of the affected population during his preaching at the various congregations. Judging from comments in the press of the time he was not reimbursed for his trouble.

The first marriage under these regulations took place at Princes Street on Wednesday 8th August 1877, Revs. M. Hast and M. Keizer of the Great Synagogue officiating. The names of the couple are not recorded. The majority of these weddings were at Princes Street, always on Wednesdays, with up to nine ceremonies in a day taking place. Problems soon arose; a member of the Board of Deputies felt they were being sidestepped but after some discussion it was decided just to ask for a copy of the regulations. Doubts about their legality, since they were taking place on premises not registered as places of worship, were dispelled by a letter, reported to the October meeting of the US council, from the Registrar General giving them full clearance.

In January of the following year a letter appeared from a guest at one of these weddings complaining of 'certain idle, rough and dirty men' inhibiting guests attending weddings at Princes Street and on one occasion some guests, he alleged, had actually been unable to reach the door. This was followed by a letter from the synagogue secretary denying the misbehaviour complained of, at the same time admitting that an unusually large crowd had gathered owing to three weddings taking place. He went on to suggest that the ceremony officials might be more punctual. A further letter from the original complainant repeated the original accusations and added that his arm was almost broken in the mêlée. Little further was heard of these cheap marriages, the exception being that on Boxing Day 1883 nine were performed at Princes Street and five at Sandys Row, the first mention of them taking place elsewhere, until June 1885 when the *Jewish Chronicle*, the *Jewish World* and *East London Advertiser* all reported a 'scandalous event'.

The previous Saturday (22nd June) a poor man, Lewis Egelowitz, had made an application to the magistrate at Thames Police Court for advice.

> He said that the Council of the United Synagogue had passed a decree offering to marry persons of the Jewish persuasion for the small fee of ten shillings and sixpence instead of the ordinary charge of three pounds fifteen and sixpence. He had taken advantage of the offer and had gone with his bride (Golda Cohen) and friends to the synagogue in Princes Street, Spitalfields to have the ceremony performed. There was a total of eight couples to be married that day and he was second on the list. The second reader, who performed the service married the first couple and charged them half-a-crown over and above the 10/6d authorised by the council. When it came to his turn the second reader demanded the extra money of him. This he refused to pay saying he was a poor man and could not pay it. The reader then ordered him and his intended bride to stand from underneath the canopy and told them to wait. He then married the other six couples. The first reader, who was present, remonstrated with his assistant saying it was cruel to keep them and punish them in that manner because they had not got the extra money to pay. The second reader then went to his desk and appeared to be fully engaged on some private matter taking no notice of the bridal pair.
>
> The first reader sent the beadle up to his colleague to come down and marry them but he refused. The first minister performed the ceremony himself according to custom reading the marriage contract and handing it to the bride's mother. At this point the second reader came under the canopy and violently snatched the document from her and put it in his pocket saying 'If you want this you must come to my office for it.' A struggle took place during which the wine cup was broken as the ceremony was being concluded and the bride's veil and dress were torn, she being pushed around.

However, the applicant was told that the event took place outside the jurisdiction of that court and he must apply to the magistrate at Worship Street. The marriages on that day were performed by the Revs. V. Rosenstein and H. Millem, first and second readers, respectively, of the East London Synagogue. The latter, who was also secretary, positively declared that the entire statement was a 'calumnious and malicious fabrication'.

Reaction was rapid; the President, Wardens and Committee of the synagogue issued a disclaimer of any part in the affair and the Honorary Officers of the United Synagogue held a special enquiry on the following Thursday, the Beth Din awaiting the result of this investigation. On 7th July, the monthly meeting of the Council took place at the Central Synagogue chambers, Great Portland Street. The chairman reported the findings of the enquiry into the behaviour of Henry Millem. All parties to the affair, including the court magistrate, the wardens of the East London Synagogue and the President of the Princes Street Synagogue had made submissions verbally or in writing and it was concluded that the reports were exaggerated and the minister himself had gained no pecuniary advantage from the extra charge. However, Rev. Millem had been guilty of rudeness and misconduct. It was recommended that he be reprimanded and required to write a letter of apology to Mr Egelowitz, the bridegroom. The secretary also read a petition signed by a hundred members of the East London Synagogue declaring that Millem should not be censured and another from the committee of the Princes Street Synagogue that a reprimand was not sufficient and that they would not allow him to officiate in future. Millem was then summoned to the council room and addressed in a very feeling manner by the Chairman who said that the present was the first occasion he had been entrusted with the painful duty of reprimanding from the chair a minister of the United Synagogue. 'Bad as Mr. Millem's conduct in disobeying the rules of the Council, his courtesy to the people he was marrying was still worse coming as it did from a minister of religion and a religion which made no distinction between rich and poor. He might consider it fortunate that those who had investigated the case thought it would be sufficient that he should only be censured and that he write a letter of apology to the aggrieved parties.' Mr Millem, while expressing regret at the occurrence and admitting that he had no fault with the decision of the Honorary Officers, declined to sign any letter of apology. At this point he withdrew from the meeting which then decided that a letter of apology be written which he would be required to sign.

This was by no means the end of the matter; to return home, Millem took an Inner Circle train to Aldgate from where he hired a cab for the short trip home. However, feeling unwell, he diverted to his physician Dr John Fordham in Mile End Road where after some treatment he expired. An inquest, which attracted considerable attention, was held the following Friday by Mr George Collier. The deceased's eldest surviving son Bernard gave evidence of identification adding that his father was aged fifty and, although in good health, had occasionally been treated by Dr Fordham; he was of a nervous disposition and tended to get agitated easily. The beadle of the East London Synagogue, Mr Abraham Winkle, stated that he had known the deceased for over twenty-five years and had found him to be a nervous and excitable person. He had last seen him alive about quarter past seven on Tuesday evening in Portland Place apparently in his usual state of health. Replying to questions about the incident at the wedding he stated that the couple were asked the usual questions and also for the half-crown cab fare. On refusing the latter, the ten and sixpence was demanded and paid. The deceased was satisfied and no further remarks made. The couple were married by the first reader who presented the certificate to the bride and the deceased asked for its return; there was no snatching but the parties of both bride and groom fell on Rev. Millem thinking he was going to run away with the document. No blows were struck but a stud fell from his breast and he made no resistance. He was excited and aggrieved. On the following Sunday he was unwell and after some minor treatment put to bed. The final witness was Dr Fordham who stated that the deceased had a feeble heart and any excitement could be dangerous. About half-past eight on Tuesday evening he arrived by cab at his house, rushing in with extended arms, and exclaiming in agonised tones that he had been unjustly accused by the Council. Two other medical men came in and, having placed him on the couch, they prescribed which seemed to give some temporary relief. He continued in a very emotional state, calling G-d to witness that he was innocent. He said, 'How shall I break the news to my wife and children?' whereupon he convulsed and died within a minute. The verdict was in accord with the medical evidence. He left a wife and eight children.

According to the *East London Advertiser* report of the inquest the 2s. 6d. cab charge had been abolished as a result of the publicity. Subsequently occasional letters appeared in the Jewish press advocating free marriages for the poor, that the marriage officials should be available on more than one day of the week and complaining of how couples were kept waiting for long periods only to have the service gabbled off at breakneck speed.

These complaints apart, nothing significant was heard about these cheap marriages until 7th November 1890 when the *Jewish World* reported that the Sandys Row Synagogue had written to the Registrar General at Somerset House, without prior reference to the United Synagogue, requesting him to stop registration of marriages at that synagogue. A meeting between the Council and synagogue officials had taken place on 9th September when five shillings per wedding was asked for so as to enable damage, alleged to have been caused by wedding guests, to be repaired. It was also stated that Princes Street Synagogue would demand the same terms. Enquiry to the latter, however, elicited the response that Sandys Row had no authority to speak on their behalf and they were willing to carry on for 2s. or 2s. 6d. The decision of the United Synagogue was to stop using both places for the cheap weddings and hold them all at the East London Synagogue. At the meeting of the Federation on Sunday 30th November the Synagogue President Leonard Read explained that though he wished to co-operate, many of these weddings took place on Sundays and since they were very close to the Sunday markets much confusion often arose. Also about £700 had recently been spent on renovations and in some cases damage had been done so that the committee thought it inadvisable to continue. The letter to the Registrar General had been withdrawn and weddings were continuing until the new arrangements were in place.

Cheap marriages continued to be held at Rectory Square until the second world war, and published figures indicated that for some of that time they accounted for over half the synagogue weddings in London with up to forty being held on a single day. A letter appeared in the *Jewish Chronicle* of 2nd October 1896 complaining of the place being remote from most people and that a compulsory offering of 2s. 6d. was being required.

Interior of Synagogue decorated for Shavuot 1911.

A Giant Among Giants

At setting of tombstone to Mark Lazarus (see p.24).

Scene in Commercial Road at funeral of Rabbi Melnick.

A Giant Among Giants

Tombstone of Rabbi Melnick.

A Giant Among Giants

Tombstone of Rabbi Melnick's mother.

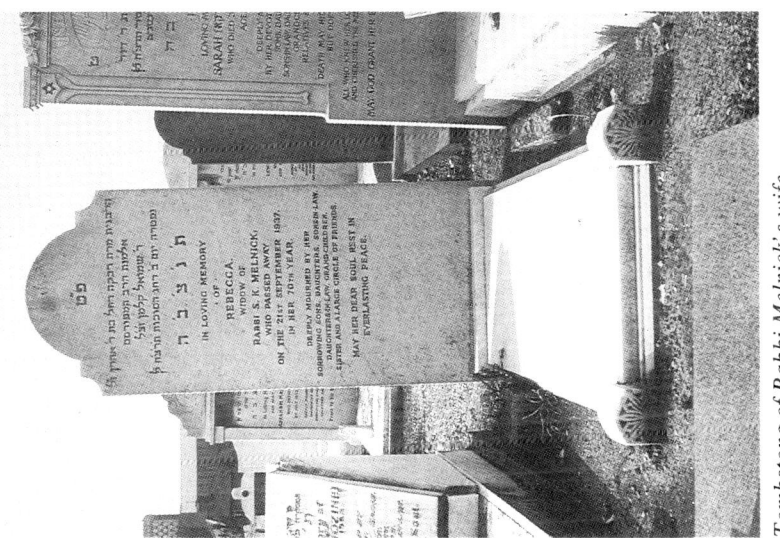

Tombstone of Rabbi Melnick's wife.

A Princes Street Synagogue Kesubah (Rabbi Melnick's daughter Rosie to Abraham Hillman).

Louisa Perina Courtauld (née Ogier) from a portrait attributed to Zoffany (permision Julien Courtauld).

Torah mantle presented by Mr L. Master for Rosh Hashana 5665 (1904) (see p.93).

Chapter 6
The Building Reconstructed

I rejoiced when they said to me, Let us go to the house of the L-rd.
Peace be within your rampart, prosperity within your palaces.
(Psalm CXXII)

Although the synagogue was well established and patronised in the main by persons of Polish origin and most of its preachers spoke in Yiddish it did not seem to have made any significant gains in membership from the influx of refugees following the assassination of Czar Alexander II in 1881. Many of its customs were reminiscent of the United Synagogue, in fact the whole organisation was modelled on the typical English style of the major synagogues and this may well have had a deterrent effect on the new immigrants. Its general business was conducted in English, another deterrent to the newcomers. Indeed its membership was falling, resulting in financial trouble, being in debt to the Loyal United Friends Benefit Society by £200. The synagogue itself was comparatively new, but the house onto which it had been built was nearly two hundred years old. There were constant problems with the roof; the wooden staircase to the ladies' gallery and, hence, to the upper floors of the house was wearing out and becoming dangerous, a similar problem was occurring with the staircase to the basement hall and the entrance door was too narrow for the safety of the people using the building. Further, ventilation left much to be desired.

The honorary architect to the Federation, Mr L. Solomon, as part of a general survey of all Federation synagogues, reported during 1892 on the building, listing the defects. Estimated cost of the recommended refurbishment was £600. A meeting of the Loyal United Friends Friendly Society on 27th November voted a £200 loan for the restoration work, to be repaid in annual instalments of £20 at 3% interest. (The outstanding loan, also of £200, from the Society was to be repaid under similar conditions after repayment of the new loan.) A request was made to the November meeting of the Federation for an appeal for the remaining £400 needed for the repairs to be launched so that the necessary work could be undertaken. The chairman of that meeting stated that it was one of the most successful in the Spitalfields area and suggested that the £100 repaid by the first of the new model synagogues, New Road, be advanced to the applicants free of interest and that a public appeal be issued by the Federation for the remainder. The loan was granted in the form of a mortgage repayable at £10 per annum. With this guarantee of funding the work was commenced in early December. A memorandum dated 10th March 1893 and placed with the deeds of the property records that Jacob Davidson of 16 Princes Square (sic), Spitalfields, the President of the synagogue, had deposited with Samuel Montague of 60 Old Broad Street in the City of London, MP, the President of the Federation of Synagogues acting on behalf of the council, the lease of the building with intent to create an equitable mortgage to secure repayment of a loan of £100. The appeal for the remaining £300 was rapidly launched in both the *Jewish Chronicle* and the *Jewish World* in their issues of 18th November 1892. The first list of donors appeared on 13th January 1893 headed by Lord Rothschild with £50 followed by Samuel Montague with thirty guineas (these and other relevant donations can still be seen inscribed on the gallery plaques) and with £100 still required. It appears that during the extensive alterations services were held in No. 17 (now 21) next door.

Thus repaired and redecorated, with frontage rebuilt with rustic arches for the windows and a matching, wide doorway for greater safety, hallway floor rebuilt in stone on iron joists and beams, concrete stairways to the gallery and basement with iron balustrades and hand rails and with a new ventilation system, the building was formally reopened on Sunday 26th March, 9th Nisan 5653 in an impressive ceremony commencing at 3 p.m. The synagogue, decorated with flowers, was declared open by Samuel Montague. The Chief Rabbi declared, in Hebrew, 'Open unto me the gates of righteousness: I will enter them and praise the L-rd', whereupon the procession consisting of himself, Rabbis Spiers and Lerner, Rev. Hast, Mr Montague, the Wardens and other Honorary Officers all bearing Scrolls, entered as the Reader, Rev. Moses Claff, assisted by a choir under the direction of Mr J. J. Bruske (of Dalston Synagogue) chanted traditional verses. Three circuits of the reading desk were made as the Reader and choir chanted Psalms XXX, C, and XXIV; Uvenucha Yomar (And when it rested he said; Numbers X 36) was sung as the Scrolls were placed in the Ark and then followed the Afternoon Service. This was followed by the dedication sermon by the Chief Rabbi:

> 'My dear brethren – I am greatly exhausted by the severe duties of yesterday for I can assure you it is no easy task to preach a sermon and a *drosha* in the Great Shool within three hours. Yet I will not refrain from testifying the interest and gratification I feel at the restoration of this synagogue. I rejoice that by the help of your brethren in faith, but mainly through your own efforts, you have been enabled to repair the breaches in this temple of prayer. I would earnestly remind you, my brethren, that this restored beauty, this outward fairness only then becomes of genuine value if it be a symbol and a pledge of the increased love and reverence, the inward earnestness and pious fear with which you purpose, henceforth to worship here the L-rd your G-d. As you look upon the outer and inner walls that have been renovated and that shine forth with radiant freshness, be admonished that you have to cleanse your minds from all disturbing thoughts, all unworthy imaginations, that you have to purge your soul from all low desires and sinful passions if you would wish that the words of your mouth and the meditation of your heart be acceptable in the sight of the L-rd your G-d. Remove the folly of idle talk, banish the plague of quarrel, discord and uncharitable and unbrotherly feeling from this sacred spot, for only then can you hope that your prayers will be accepted in mercy by the Father of Mercy.
>
> 'Yet, momentous though these considerations be, it is not my intention to dwell on them this day. I would rather speak to you on what I consider to be the duty of the hour, on your attitude, your obligations to brethren who have newly arrived here from the country where they have been so cruelly oppressed and so heartlessly persecuted. How shall I act towards these hapless refugees from Russian tyranny? shall we join the hue and cry which is raised in certain quarters and signify our assent to any measures that may prevent the immigration of 'destitute aliens' as they are called? shall we turn away from them with cold disdain so that they may speedily quit the place which shows them such scant hospitality? No, my brethren, emphatically no! Our conduct is clearly prescribed by the words of Torah (Exodus XXII 9): 'Thou shalt not oppress a stranger for ye know the heart of a stranger seeing that ye were strangers in the land of Egypt.'
>
> Selfishness, lack of sympathy with those wretched outcasts, is altogether unworthy of a human being. With us Jews it would be altogether inexplicable. Shall we, whose ancestors suffered in the land of Egypt, shall we allow no fellow feeling with our brethren who have just escaped from bondage? And if the remembrances of Egyptian serfdom leave you cold and unimpressed, do not the words of our text vividly recall to you what is fully within your recollection? Is then the time so very distinct when you passed anxious lives yourselves within the inhospitable lands of the north? Is it then so many years ago that you came to this country as a 'greener' yourself, not having even the traditional half-crown in your pocket? Should you then not know the heart of the stranger?

There are few points on which the Bible insists with greater emphasis than on the duty we owe to the foreigner. Our Rabbis lay stress on the fact that the Torah warns us of our duty to the stranger and foreigner in as many as thirty-six different passages. What is your primary obligation to the unfortunate refugees who have sought these shores? 'Thou shalt not oppress the stranger!' We hear it said now and again that there are certain employers of labour, tailors and bootmakers; cabinet makers and tobacco manufacturers who take advantage of the poor 'greener' when he comes here, homeless, friendless and helpless, to make him work for the very lowest wage which will keep body and soul together, aye, even for less, the employers thinking that some of our charities or that some of the charitable members of our community will not permit the man to starve. I earnestly hope that none of you are guilty of this grievous sin. I hope and believe that the sweating system no longer exists as a system, though I fear that individual instances are still but too plentiful. There are still too many manufacturers who, themselves, or through their managers, use every pretext in order to cut down payment for work and treat those who are within their power with insult and contempt. Oh! if there be those guilty of such conduct, will they not listen to the denunciation of the divine prophet (Isaiah III 14, 15) 'The spoil of the poor is in your houses. What mean ye that crush my people and grind the faces of the poor, saith the L-rd G-d of Hosts'. It is also a source of keen and bitter regret to hear that through the greed, perhaps also through want of management on the part of employers, there are too many of our poor workmen who are driven to desecrate Sabbath and Festival. Can there be a grosser offence than this?

All these, however, are negative duties. But you have also positive obligations to the poor humble 'greener'. We shall read in the Festival lesson on Sabbath next, 'And when a stranger sojourneth with thee and he desireth to keep the Passover of the L-rd,' he was first to be naturalised by means of entering the covenant of Abraham, then let him come near and keep it, and he shall be as one born in the land. Now the readiest means of naturalisation is learning the language of the country in which we have elected to settle. I hope that you will join your efforts to ours with the view of inducing your workmen to attend the evening classes established at the Free School and in various Board schools for the purpose of learning English. And let it be your care that with the language he should also acquire English modes of thought, English standards of cleanliness, decency and straightforwardness, and, especially, a deep and abiding respect for law. 'One law shall be to him that is homeborn and unto the stranger that sojourneth among you'. By your example and by your admonition you must impress upon him the lesson that he dare not to transgress or to evade the laws of the land, and the laws framed by any constituted authority whether it be the County Council or the vestry, the United Synagogue or the Federation and being the object of all these laws not to annoy and to hamper but to protect and to assist them in gaining their daily bread and to enable them to dwell in safety with peace and with honour in the land.

There are, unfortunately, a certain number, I hope and believe it is a few among the dwellers in the East, who through poverty, ignorance and discontent with their sad lot yield to the enticement of evil tempters and turn their back on their holy religion, who frequent anarchy and revolutionary clubs and who become tainted with the pestilential doctrines they set forth. You must feel it your duty to prevent workmen from being thus ensnared and you must seek the rescue of them when they are in danger of being beguiled. Both by your example and by your admonition you must keep them away from gambling dens and tell them they should worthily use their leisure by resorting to evening classes, to working men's clubs, the free public library, and by attending lectures and meetings calculated to promote their moral and religious welfare.

You have already proved your willingness to further these ends by the kind alacrity with which you have offered your commodious rooms for the meetings of the Sabbath Observance Leagues. In the tablet which hangs there recording the benefactors to your synagogue, I note that you describe yourselves as the Loyal United Friends Friendly Society. This title aptly summarises the duties you owe to the poor 'greener'. Strive to render them loyal to their G-d, their faith and their country. Prove yourselves sincere friends to them, unite with them a common faith, a common country of birth, a common country of adoption. If you do this then will your assemblies of public worship be a freewill offering of love and devotion, which will be accepted with grace and in mercy by our Father in Heaven.

The Chief Rabbi concluded with a prayer:

Oh L-rd G-d ever merciful and gracious, unto Thee do we lift up our soul. We yield our heartfelt thanks unto Thee that Thou hast blessed the work of our hands and enabled us to save and again to consecrate this building to the honour and glory of Thee, who dwellest among the praises of Israel. Grant that this synagogue may ever remain a centre of peace and union and brotherhood, a centre of pious and virtuous life. Fill us with Thy spirit that we may raise hands and hearts to Thee, asking Thee what wouldst thou have me to do. Here am I, send me.

Vouchsafe Thy glorious blessing unto Thy servant who has reopened this house, unto all who have laboured for its restoration, unto all whose heart hast stirred them up to their gladsome offerings.

Thou on Whose gracious providence we evermore depend, shield and protect our Queen and Her Royal house. Bless this country and grant it true and abiding prosperity. Do thou direct and prosper the consultations of those assembled in the high court of parliament for the safety, honour and welfare of our Sovereign and Her dominions. Thou who didst ransom Thy people Israel with a mighty hand and an outstretched arm in time past, be with those who are still trodden down beneath the iron hoof of bigotry and despotism. May this Passover-tide be a season of freedom and herald deliverance to tens and hundreds of thousands of stricken lives. Thou hast vouchsafed Thy gracious promise, I will be as the dew unto Israel. Revive us with the dew of Thy heavenly mercy so that Israel may grow as the lily and cast forth its roots as the Lebanon that we may stand forth among the nations in purest moral beauty and holiness, in renewed freshness and intensified strength. Amen.

Following the prayer for the Royal Family, the announcement of donations and prayer for the donors, the service concluded with Oleinu, Psalm CL and Yigdal. Mr Davidson presented Mr Montague with a handsomely bound copy of the order of service and a key of the synagogue. It might be considered relevant at this point to note that among the donations recorded on the panels of the ladies' gallery is one of £1 1s. 0d. from H. Bawtree, clearly the freeholder. (Henry Bawtree died two years later, the property passing to Lawrence Bawtree Meredith of Croydon.) An innovation coinciding with the reconstruction was the formation of a Ladies' Holy Vestment Society for providing furnishings for the synagogue and assisting persons in need.

In July the street was renamed Princelet Street and the synagogue, which had just become officially the Princes Street Synagogue added, in parenthesis, 'now Princelet' to its name; this designation surviving until 1918 when the Princes Street name was officially dropped. With the ceremony over, a new problem arose not to be finally settled for almost two years. Rev. Claff, reader since Rosh Hashanah 1887, had decided to accept the offer of the corresponding post at the New Road Synagogue and resigned. The first of a long series of guest readers was Kolman Davies of Warsaw, a nephew of Rev. Hast of the Great followed by I. M. Friedlander during Shavuot, Dayan Spiers giving the address on the first day of the festival. Still maintaining his contact with the congregation Alexander Tertis celebrated the barmitzvah of his son Samuel on 1st July inviting all to the subsequent reception in the afternoon. Another loss was that of Abraham Heisser as secretary, he being replaced by Isaac Kaliski, already secretary of the Chevra Tehillim and a host of other organisations. The organisation almost lost its president who, with some difficulty, was persuaded to remain in office. Back at a Federation meeting in May Davidson proposed a motion which was carried unanimously that cheap synagogues should be established further east so as to relieve the pressure on those in the Spitalfields area. Still trying to find a new reader, further guest appearances included Revs. H. Caplan, M. L. Cohen of the Borough Synagogue, and M. Bregman from Northampton during the High Festivals. The newly elected Dayan Sussman Cohen gave the address on 12th August.

At the committee meeting of 14th January 1894 it was announced that £100 in contributions and offerings were still owing and that this could lead to closure of the Shool. At a meeting a fortnight later it was decided to give sick pay by the day, that *shiva* benefits for members of Society and Synagogue would be £2 16s. 0d, Society only £2 2s. 0d. and Synagogue only 15s. During February a short list of Messrs. Cohen, Davies, Myers and Wiseman was drawn up of whom the last named was elected *chazan* at the Annual meeting during April. Some six weeks later he announced he was to get married and a fund for a present started with 10s. 6d. from Jacob Davidson. Shortly after this, he left and a Mr Mittleburg, who had just arrived from Berlin, was suggested as a possible successor. Following a single service he was taken on, on a temporary basis, at £1 per week and £5 for the High Festivals. On 19th May Rabbi Lerner, newly appointed rabbi of the Federation, preached.

For the High Festivals 'the synagogue was filled to overflowing', services being conducted by Rev. Mittleburg assisted by Mr Generzan. The address on Kol Nidre was given by Rev. Isidore Myers who discussed the verse 'For on that day shall the priest make an atonement for you,' (Leviticus XVI 30). Soon Mittleburg was asking for more money; having started at £1 he wanted an extra five shillings a week and £10 for the festivals; this was not acceptable and he was given notice expiring on 4th November to which he countered by announcing he was to get married and handed in his resignation effective 4th November.

In September the Ladies' Society presented two silver breast plates costing £30 at a service conducted by Rev Mittleburg and addressed by Rabbi Cohen. It appears that a row with the *chazan* developed at this service which led to the events mentioned above.

On 9th November one of the founder members, Simon Goldberg, died at the age of sixty after a short illness. He had been an officer of the Chevra Tehillim and was an uncle of Mrs Kaliski, wife of the secretary.

The vacancy for a *chazan* was eventually filled by Philip Fassenfeld during February 1895; Wiseman, trying for a second term, having been rejected. The election of the new *chazan* brought a period of stability to the office but the financial positions of both synagogue and society were worsening and amalgamation with the Konin Synagogue of 84 Hanbury Street was being considered; negotiations, although they reached an advanced state, appear to have been abortive.

The major event of the year, despite the financial problems, was the celebration of the silver jubilee of the synagogue organised by the Ladies' Society for Providing Holy Vestments. It took place on 8th September and involved the presentation of a new Scroll by Mrs Rachel Abrahams of Mansell Street and silver breast plate by the Ladies' Society. After the writing of the last verse had been completed, the Afternoon Service was read by Rev. Fassenfeld assisted by a choir and was followed by the presentation of the silver breast plate for the Scroll by Mrs Adler, President of the Ladies' Society. The synagogue president then thanked the donors for their gifts and the choir sang Psalm XXIV. At this point Dayan Spiers delivered an hour-long discourse in Yiddish. In it he compared the current celebration with that in Germany which marked the twenty-fifth anniversary of the end of the Franco-Prussian war as he had done that many years ago at the original consecration, quoting the Psalm (XX), 'Some trust in chariots and some in horses; but we will remember the name of the L-rd our G-d.' He then went on to show how the three events they were celebrating that day were suggested in the portion read the previous day. When the farmer brought, in joy, his first ripe fruits to the Temple he was not to forget his humble origins; '"A Syrian ready to perish was my father and he went down to Egypt and sojourned there, few in number." (Deut. XXVI, 5). You also should remember how, starting only a few in number to worship in a small room you had, with the help of Providence, prospered and grown from strength to strength until at last you had been kept alive and enabled to reach this happy season to see this joyful anniversary of the foundation.' Secondly, quoting verse 11: '"And you shall rejoice in all the good which has been done to you" etc. for there is nothing good except the Torah and it is our duty to rejoice in it just as you are consecrating today a new Sepher Torah but not just this but also diligently studying and observing all its teachings and by teaching it to your children.' His third simile involved the second part of the verse, 'and unto your house' this term being explained as meaning your wife. By taking an interest in synagogue affairs and founding a society for providing holy vestments whose fine gifts were being presented that day, the ladies had proved themselves true daughters of Israel and worthy descendants of Sarah, Miriam and Deborah and all the great Hebrew women of old. Finally he concluded with a prayer specially composed by himself for the occasion. He was followed by Michael Adler who told the assembly to be proud of their pretty place of worship. It had grown from a tiny *chevra* and could not grow too large. He recalled his boyhood, remembered his barmitzvah there and was pleased to see many of the old faces but was grieved by absences; those who had passed on should not be forgotten. He was glad to see the interest the Ladies' Society took in the synagogue and although himself no longer a member, he praised their efforts (his mother being the president) for the handsome gifts just presented. 'A synagogue that was conducted in a proper orthodox manner was far better than another that had fine ornaments and no proper service.' He considered the present a very joyful occasion. The congregation then adjourned to the Criterion Club in Hanbury Street for refreshments and the usual self-congratulatory speeches.

From the joy of this ceremony, the solemnity of the High Festivals and the rejoicing of Succoth came tragedy. There is no record of the circumstances or even the actual event in the press. The first mention of it to be found in both papers was in the issues of 3rd January 1896 where we are informed that 'Rev. Elias Regensberg delivered a sermon on Sunday in memory of the late Rev. Louis Cohen who was, for many years, Rabbi to this (Princes Street) Synagogue.' For any further detail we have to turn to the account book of the Chevra Tehillim which informs us that on 2nd December 1895 £2 14s. 6d. was spent on coaches and cabs at the funeral of the late rabbi and we have to look even further ahead to discover that the interment was at West Ham Cemetery. Another entry in the same book was for payment of ten shillings to 'Rev. S. Melnik for services' on 31st December. Whether he took part in the memorial service or took over some of the deceased's duties is a matter for speculation.

A further entry in the same book, this time dated 29th March 1896 informs us that Rabbi Melnick was paid £1 as salary for two weeks but it was not until 17th April that an announcement of the appointment appeared in the press to which was added, 'Tehillim is chanted every Sabbath at 1 p.m. and also expounded by the Rabbi two hours prior to the Evening Service.' Thus began his long association with the Chevra Tehillim and synagogue. Another item recorded in the accounts was the payment of one shilling for clearing the former rabbi's books. The new rabbi was being paid one shilling per week more than his predecessor whose own salary had risen from six shillings since 1888. In July this was increased to fourteen shillings at the same time as that of the reader was raised from £1 to 25 shillings. At the same meeting the Chevra Torah (then of 30 Hanbury Street) was given permission to use the premises when not required by the Society or Chevra Tehillim, at five shillings per week. A week later on 14th July a letter from Jacob Davidson was received stating that he could no longer carry on as president in the proper manner and Philip Silverstone was elected in his place. Jacob Davidson appears to have paid his synagogue dues up to the end of November 1897 but then, no further. Finally, at the end of this same eventful month, the Kamenitzer Maggid gave the address at the barmitzvah of the secretary's elder son. A month later on 30th August the Ladies' Society made yet another presentation, this time of a silk Ark curtain embroidered in gold with matching covers for the reader's desk, lectern and a mantle for a Sepher Torah to a total value of £40. The service was conducted by Rev. Fassenfeld and addressed by Rabbis Melnick and Orliansky (of the Chevra Torah) followed by refreshments in the vestry room. This was the same day as the opening of the new Great Garden Street Synagogue.

Arrangements for the High Holiday services were that Mr Grozen would assist the reader, the rabbi to the Chevra Tehillim would speak on the first day of Rosh Hashanah for a fee of 10s. 6d, seats would be available at 3s., 4s., 5s., and 6s.; gallery at 3s.; for strangers from 5s. at the back and on chairs 3s. Two extra beadles would be employed for 10s. and 5s. respectively. Rabbi Melnick was also to lecture on first day Succoth (no fee for this sermon is stated). The committee meeting of 18th October had two major items on its agenda. First was the resignation of 'Mr Harris' as *shammas* and collector in return for which it was decided that he should receive £44 in cash, retain his living rooms and remain as caretaker for a fee of £2 per annum; secondly the secretary was instructed to apply to the Board of Deputies for a certificate as marriage secretary. The vacancy for a beadle was not advertised for a month when it appeared twice, while the committee decided that the successful candidate was to be paid £20 per annum plus 2½% on collections and 1s. entrance fee for society and synagogue or 6d. synagogue only. According to the minute book there were eight applicants of whom David Davitzky was elected to the post with 25 votes, duties to commence on 4th January 1897, the runner-up being Mr Brodetzky with 13. His son Professor Selig Brodetzky in his book *Memoirs: From Ghetto to Israel* states that his father 'was the *shammas* of a small synagogue in Princelet Street with a weekly salary of less than a pound a week.' The full description is plainly of our synagogue but the record in the minute book clearly indicates that he failed to obtain the appointment.

The committee meeting of 20th December was informed that a meeting had taken place with the Chevra Konin (84 Hanbury Street) and for the second time it was proposed that amalgamation, subject to certain conditions, take place. The *chevra* had about 40 members, 8 scrolls, £40 in cash assets, and silver ornaments to the value of £60. This amalgamation, once again, does not appear to have come to fruition.

At the committee meeting of 23rd January 1897 it was announced that the Board of Deputies had appointed Isaac Kaliski as Marriage Secretary and, consequently, marriages could be conducted there. Marriage fee, initially, was to be 25s. but evidently was reduced to one guinea before being publicised by announcements in the Yiddish press at weekly intervals. It was also decided to hold a special service on the following Sunday in aid of the Chief Rabbi's appeal on behalf of the Indian Famine Fund, with Rabbi Melnick as the preacher. The service raised £4 for the fund. Another matter was disagreement between the new *shammas* and 'Mr Harris', the latter to be asked to leave the premises on consideration of an extra 6s. per week. A gift of *tallesim* from the Ladies' Society was also acknowledged.

Consecration of the memorial stone for the late Rabbi Cohen of the Chevra Tehillim of Princes Street Synagogue and of Mile End New Town Synagogue took place on Sunday 17th January at West Ham Cemetery, his successor Rabbi Melnick giving the address.

The first marriage under the synagogue's own auspices was solemnised on 16 June, being the wedding of Rabbi Maccoby's daughter Milly to Davis Polliabshek. The following Sunday, in celebration of the golden jubilee of Queen Victoria, Rabbi Orliansky preached at the service which commenced at 6 p.m. A month later a meeting was held in connection with the proposed Zionist congress to be held later that year, a week after a memorial service for the late Rabbi Yoffey of Manchester at a full synagogue with many unable to enter. Rabbi Orliansky was once again the preacher. In early November study of the Book of Psalms under Rabbi Melnick was completed and this was celebrated in traditional fashion under the chairmanship of Mark Moses, President of the Chevra Tehillim. At the same meeting a presentation of a Kiddush cup was made to 'Mr Harris' with the inscription:

> 'Presented by the Committee of the Chevroth Tehillim Umishmorim to Mr. Harris Levy as a small mark of esteem for his valuable services as Founder and Warden, 6th November 1897 – 11th Cheshvan 5658.'

General meetings around this time showed synagogue membership to be about 90 and *chevra* membership about 100. The low synagogue membership precipitated another amalgamation process, this time successfully, with the Chevra Mikra of 46 New Court, Fashion Street. A meeting on 12th December chaired by Philip Silverstone with the visiting delegation led by its President Mr H. Goldberg and a trustee Mr J. Weber agreed terms and decided that formal union should take place on Shevat 15th 5658, 6th February 1898, that the congregation would be known as the Chevra Mikra U'nedivath Chein, and that they would bring 4 scrolls, 4 silver breast plates, 2 sets of bells, 1 crown, 7 pointers, 5 Ark curtains, 12 mantles, 1 silver and 1 brass basins (to be used alternately on festivals), a silver cup and spice box, brass candlestick, *megillah* and *shofar*. The membership of the Fashion Street Synagogue would be transferred to Princelet Street together with all the books in addition to the articles mentioned. There were also to be nine procedural conditions. Rabbi Melnick would preach at the ceremony. Despite the original agreement the amalgamation took place on Sunday 30th January when the Officers of the Chevra Mikra carried the Scrolls in procession to Princelet Street to be met in the vestibule by the receiving officers also carrying Scrolls, all then making three circuits of the *bimah* while traditional verses and Psalms were recited by Rev. Fassenfeld. The Scrolls were deposited in the Ark and the Afternoon Service read. Rabbi Melnick then gave a lengthy oration in which he praised the officers of the two synagogues for their foresight and mutual trust in bringing about a union which preserved the best traditions of both parties. This was followed by a celebratory supper in the vestry hall with further speeches. The following Shabbat, Dayan Sussman Cohen preached on the subject of falsehood. Meanwhile the Ladies' Holy Vestment Society was making good headway with income of £65 15s. 2d. and it was decided to distribute some of this among the poor for Pesach. One of the traditions brought from the Chevra Mikra was the celebration of the anniversary of the traditional date of the birth and death of Moses the Lawgiver on 7th Adar with sermons at the afternoon service followed by a celebratory meal. On this first joint occasion, 1st March, the service which commenced at 4 o'clock was conducted by Rev. Fassenfeld with orations by Dayanim Spiers and Sussman Cohen and Rabbi Lipman, and included a *hesped* for the late Britzker Rav. This was followed by supper at 2s. 6d. a head, presided over by the President Philip Silverstone and the several speakers included Rabbi David Kohn Zedek. On 19th March the Chief Rabbi addressed a full attendance on the sanctity of work and the necessity of apprenticing children to trades which were not overcrowded. He drew attention to the efforts of the Board of Guardians and the Sabbath Observance Bureau and pleaded for masters and men to bring about better observance of the Holydays. Finally he addressed Albert Kaliski, second son of the secretary, who was celebrating his barmitzvah that day.

After a short illness Coleman Angel, one of the founders of both Society and Synagogue, died on Saturday 13th August aged sixty-five, leaving a widow, two sons and four daughters. The funeral was at Plashet cemetery and tombstone was set during the following April. At the next committee meeting a letter of condolence was sent to the family. A sign of the poverty of the synagogue occurred at the same meeting when it was announced that repairs to several scrolls would cost £7, the Ladies' Society being asked to meet the expense. At the next meeting six guineas were voted for a choir for the High Festivals and it was decided that members were to be charged sixpence per quarter for a Simchat Torah fund, thus allowing everyone the honour of being chosen as *chosan*. The opening of the Spitalfields Great Synagogue by the Chevra Machzike Hadass v'Shomrei Shabbat on 11th September, one week later than originally planned, was a major carnival event with several local synagogues assisting, including Princelet Street with the loan of its *chupah*. An innovation of the year was the placing of plates by the Chovevi Zion in a number of synagogues on Yom Kippur to collect money for poor colonists in Palestine. A total of £17 13s. 3d. was donated that year to the society of which 4s. 2d. came from Princelet Street. The October committee meeting authorised the use of the hall and committee room by the Wilna Benevolent fund for four guineas a year and allowed the reader an additional three guineas for his choir.

At a general meeting during November membership was reported to have increased to 140 with income reported at a little below £389 and expenditure according to the *Jewish Chronicle* of £341 and the *Jewish World* as £353. A special meeting of the Society in mid-December confirmed that the lease of the premises belonged to itself as long as the synagogue was in its debt: a meeting of the synagogue committee of the same date (and almost the same personnel) decided to reduce that debt by £50.

Use of the hall and committee room on Monday nights was granted to the Union of Peace Benefit Divisional Society of Hackney Downs on 5th February for a rental of one guinea a quarter. At the same meeting the collector was allowed one and a half guineas as he had been robbed of his clothes. The Ladies' Society held their annual meeting at this time, Mrs Adler reporting that relief had been given to 170 families over the past two years and that £20 had been set aside for distribution during the coming Passover period.

The next 7th Adar service was on 19th February when there seemed to be some last minute changes in speakers; as we read in chapter 2 Rabbi Newman took the place of Rabbi Lipman, and Dayan Spiers did not speak as advertised. The service was followed by a banquet at the Criterion Club in Hanbury Street (according to the *Jewish World*) or Hackney Road (*Jewish Chronicle*), cost being 3s. for one or 5s. for husband and wife. The Pesach services were conducted by Rabbi Melnick in the absence of Rev. Fassenteld for which he was paid one guinea. In addition he preached on both the first and the seventh days. During April the Tailors' Mutual Friendly Society was given permission to use the hall, as before, at one guinea a quarter.

After several months' illness Harris Levy (Mr Harris), one of the founders of the Society and Synagogue and founder of the Chevra Tehillim, died on 17th July. Harris Levy had been born on the Russian/Prussian frontier in 1813 and came to England during 1849. In addition to the three synagogue organisations, he was instrumental in the formation of the East London Jewish Male and Female Benevolent and Burial Society, and assisted the Marriage Portion Society, the Confined Mourning (*Shiva*) and Burial Society, the Talmud Torah and many other similar organisations; many newcomers to the country were referred to him for assistance in finding relatives and frequently obtaining finance to help them in their first few weeks. He was described as 'the poor man's almoner relieving the distress of the poor through the proceeds of the charity of the poor.' For almost the whole of this time he was *shammas* of the synagogue he had helped to found. His funeral at Plashet was attended by a large number of mourners.

Prior to New Year 5660 (1899) the synagogue was redecorated and Mr Rosinski, as in the previous year, assisted Rev. Fassenfeld with the services. Following complaints from the Charity Commissioners, new trustees were appointed at the December General meeting to be Philip Silverstone, Hyam Solomon and M. Smith. At the same meeting a motion to subscribe sixpence per year per member to the funds of the Federation was passed, despite a working deficit over the year of £14. This being the period of the Boer war, an appeal on behalf of the Lord Mayor's Soldiers' Widows and Orphans Fund raised five guineas. The wardens were also empowered to spend certain amounts for charitable purposes. The annual general meeting of the Loyal United Friends Friendly Society immediately followed that of the synagogue, as was normal practice, and its officers were instructed to take steps to reorganise the Society. A week later, at the age of forty-five, the death occurred of Hannah, wife of Mark Moses, President of the Chevra Tehillim and mother of Miriam Moses, sometime Mayor of the Metropolitan Borough of Stepney and a noted social worker in both the Jewish and general communities.

The final year of the century did not begin in an auspicious manner for on 1st January Phoebe, wife of Rev. Tertis, former reader, died followed on the next day by Joseph Adler. Only six weeks later on 18th February yet another death, this time of Sarah Fassenfeld aged only thirty-one, wife of the present reader, occurred. It appears she died following the birth of a son since the *Jewish Express* in its issue of 9th February records that at the Brith Milah of the son (named Abraham) of Rev. Fassenfeld 21s. were collected for Brick Lane Talmud Torah by the President of the Princelet Street Shool, Rev. Tertis being the *Mohel*. However the baby only survived a few months. A second collection on behalf of the victims of the war in the name of the Queen resulted in a further five guineas being raised by the membership. New rules for the synagogue were read out at the committee meeting on 7th January and were approved for printing and circulation (no copies have been found and are not detailed in the minutes). Meanwhile the Chevra Tehillim with a membership of 375 raised its subscription to three pence a week, *shiva* benefit to two guineas, member's death benefit to £6 and wife's death benefit to £4.

The annual meeting of the Ladies' Society took place at the end of February, the President Mrs Adler being absent (presumably owing to the recent death of her husband). It was reported that financial assistance had been given to about 900 people during the past year and £20 had been set aside for similar use over the coming Pesach period. The annual 7th Adar service was held on 11th March (II Adar 10) when Dayanim Spiers and Sussman Cohen and Rabbis Lipman and Melnick gave the addresses; these included a memorial for Rabbi I. H. Levenson of Leeds who had died the previous week. The service was followed by a supper in the vestry hall, presided over in what was to be his last public function by Philip Silverstone whilst Dayan Spiers remarked that he was pleased the amalgamation had been a success. The crowded Passover services, conducted as usual by Rev. Fassenfeld, took on a mournful tone when the President was taken ill and died aged only fifty on the last day, leaving a widow and eight children. (Philip Silverstone had come to England from Poltusk (Russia), quickly establishing himself as a communal worker. In addition to the synagogue presidency he was a member of both societies attached to it, vice-president of the Sabbath Meals Society, a founder and trustee of the Fieldgate Street Synagogue, delegate to the Federation Burial Society and subscriber to a large number of charities as well as being a member of the North London (United) Synagogue near his home at 288 Upper Street, Islington.) Eulogies at the funeral at Edmonton cemetery were given by Rabbis Melnick and Maccoby and the service conducted by Rev. Fassenfeld, the ministers of the North London synagogue also being present. A special committee meeting was held the following Sunday to express regret and condolences to the family. Tombstone was consecrated on Sunday 5th August only a week after that of Harris Levy at Plashet.

Meanwhile in May the Federation reported rules for medical provision for its members, Princelet Street with its two societies providing such a service being among those voting against. The committee meetings of 19th August were told that £350 was now owed by the synagogue to the Society suggesting that it was £20 behind with its agreed repayments. On 11th September Rev. Fassenfeld married Leah Cohen at Princelet Street, the officiants being Revs. J. Rosenzweig of Bangor and A. Perlzweig of Vine Court Synagogue. He was presented with a silver *kiddush* cup and a pair of silver candlesticks by the members. Towards the end of the year several presentations were made to the synagogue including silk mantles, an Ark curtain and on Chanukah a silver *menorah*. This last was at a special service conducted by Rev. Fassenfeld with choir and addressed by Rabbi Melnick followed by refreshments and entertainments by the committee and overseen by the recently elected President Samuel Barnett who proposed a vote of thanks to the ladies for their handsome gift. The report in the *Jewish World* of 28th December added that the society had a membership of about three hundred and that two-thirds of its income was distributed among the poor for the Holydays. Thus the century ended on a high note, perhaps thought not possible at the beginning of the year.

Chapter 7

The Early Twentieth Century

Fear the L-rd and the king, my son and do not meddle with those given to change.
(Proverbs XXIV 21)

The new century started in much the same way as the previous one finished but it was to see changes so dramatic that volumes have been written in description yet no one has fully come to terms with them: two world wars; the Russian revolution; the foundation of an independent Jewish state – Israel; the overthrow of Communist domination of Eastern Europe. Indeed as I write more great changes are occurring.

For the Princelet Street Synagogue everything began where it had left off the previous year; by its centenary, having absorbed several, it had itself amalgamated with another, that soon to close its doors.

The annual meeting of the Chevra Tehillim was held in early January with no significant change in personnel; it was the end of that month that signalled the start of change. The death of Queen Victoria on 22nd January, although not unexpected, nevertheless came as a shock to the country. Among the synagogues, preachers at the morning prayers who paid their tributes, here it was Reb Shmuel Kalman, and memorial services were hastily arranged for the termination of Shabbat at 5.30; at Princelet Street the service was conducted by Rev. Fassenfeld with the sermon preached by Rabbi Hyman Shulman. Next day a special meeting decided to send a letter of condolence to the new King and the Royal Family; a reply being received during March. In August £2 was donated to the Queen Victoria memorial fund.

In the meantime the Ladies' Society held its annual meeting at which it was reported that a hundred families had been helped during the past year and £20 was to be distributed for the coming Passover.

The committee meeting of 14th July considered a complaint about a smell of gas. A fitter had recommended that the piping be renewed but the decision was to investigate the use of electricity for lighting and a sub-committee to look into the matter was appointed. The need for a new kitchen range was also discussed. Another item raised at this same meeting was an application from Rev. Fassenfeld to become a *Mohel*. He was told to raise a petition and apply to the Chief Rabbi. Despite the entry in the account book in 1897 of the expenditure of one shilling for the removal of the late Rabbi Cohen's books the November meeting was told that those books were to be catalogued, with all three organisations sharing the cost. A decision on their future would be taken at a later date. The Gemilluth Chassodim Society of the Federation of Synagogues held its annual service at Princelet Street on Sunday 1st December, this being conducted by Rev. Fassenfeld and addressed by Rabbi Maccoby. The occasion was particularly notable since the decision earlier to investigate the use of electric light had come to fruition and the new medium was put into use for the first time, one of the first synagogues to use it. (Cost of the new lighting was to be the subject of an appeal to the membership and the Ladies' Society was asked for a contribution, a donation of £15 being forthcoming. It must be presumed that the entire cost was defrayed in this manner as no such item appears in the regular accounts.) Mark Silverstone donated the Ner Tamid in memory of his father Philip (the previous president). The fittings removed as a result of this change were sold for 10 shillings, presumably for scrap, the following year.

The next committee meeting allowed use of the committee room by the Tradesmen's Divisional Society on Sundays from 6 to 7.30 p.m. at three guineas a quarter. Owing to heavy expenses during the past year there was no surplus by the synagogue although the Society had a £10 excess. The Chevra Tehillim also showed a loss over the year, partly due to the demise of nine members, including a former Vice-president, Abraham Goldman, the largest number in its twenty-eight years' history. At this meeting Jacob Davidson announced his resignation as treasurer, a post he had held since its formation. Subsequent to this he seems to have faded out, no further reference to him being found in any of the records of the three organisations although the Post Office directory appears to record that his business was at 16, only, Princelet Street from 1900 to 1901 and subsequently at Kingsland and Pimlico to 1904 after which he seems to be lost to the records.

The February 1902 meeting allocated a room for two hours daily for Rabbi Chaikin to conduct a study circle: details published in May were

8-10 p.m. Monday to Thursday and 6-8 p.m. Sundays, Shulchan Orach being studied. The annual 7th Adar service was addressed by Rabbis Melnick, Chaikin and a newcomer, David Kohn Zedek, son of Joseph Kohn Zedek. During May a new offshoot of the Federation of Synagogues known as the Jewish Congregational Union was formed. Its principal object was to spread the Federation among the various provincial communities and Princelet Street was represented at the inaugural meeting by Messrs J. Marks, Samuel Barnett, Lazarus Solomon, and H. S. Davis. It did achieve somewhat more success than a similar but rather less ambitious initiative by the United Synagogue but it was abandoned after about three years, the Provincial communities preferring to retain their independence of London.

At the end of the month Mrs Fassenfeld gave birth to a daughter. The coronation of the new King Edward VII had been arranged for Saturday 5th July but he became ill and the ceremony had to be postponed: Psalms were said daily at Princelet Street after the morning service for his recovery and on Sabbath a special prayer was intoned. The coronation finally took place on 9th August when the special prayer composed by the Chief Rabbi was recited by Rev. Fassenfeld. On 12th October a special general meeting of the Society was held to devise a plan of reorganisation and to induce new members to join; at the same time it was decided to reduce the brightness of the electric lighting by half at a cost of £2 5s. 9d.

The High Festival services presented no diversions and it was not until the annual get-together on Shemini Atzeret to honour the bridegrooms Messrs A. Lublinsky and B. Rabinowitz that anything untoward occurred. The assemblage was chaired by the President and after the loyal toast and toasts to the honoured gentlemen it was realised that the Rabbi of the Chevra Tehillim was not present. It subsequently transpired that the secretary had forgotten to send an invitation, for which he apologised at the next committee meeting and was instructed to send an appropriately worded letter of regret. The next meeting heard a complaint against the reader for 'refractory conduct' and he was required to apologise to the chairman. Other decisions at this same meeting were to fix a heating stove in the synagogue and that the wardens should have the keys to the charity boxes. The annual meeting took place on 14th December when it was announced that all gratuities and offerings to officials were to be abolished; the beadle and collector was to be dismissed and his place taken temporarily by Aaron Seratsky. The annual meeting of the Society followed immediately after; Samuel Barnett, Frits Falkenstein and Moses Joel being elected President, Vice-president and Treasurer, respectively, of both organisations. In addition the synagogue wardens were M. Kutner and H. Goldberg. The dismissed beadle was given £5 compensation and the vacancy advertised in the *Jewish World*. The next beadle was Mr J. Miller, who was to receive £15 a year for synagogue duties and £10 for the society plus $2\frac{1}{2}$% commission, together with free rooms at least until December. In the meantime Rev. Fassenfeld was given three months notice after failing to examine all but one of the Scrolls; by 1st March the row had been patched up and he was re-elected by 36 votes to 7. The annual meeting of the Ladies' Society reported that £41 had been distributed in relief during the past year and to a greater number of people than previously and that £25 was available for Passover distribution in the current year. The remaining annual meeting was of the Chevra Tehillim with Mark Moses as President and Moses Joel Vice-president. Mr M. Barnett was presented with a pair of silver candlesticks in recognition of his many years' service as warden.

On the first day of Pesach 1903 the *Daily News*, as part of a London wide study of attendances at various religious establishments, carried out a survey of the numbers attending the various synagogue services in the capital. Attendances at sixty-five establishments, thirty-eight of them in Stepney and the City of London, were recorded; numbers of men, women and children are listed separately with the total attendance for each place. In some places the total attendance given exceeded the accommodation available; at 18 Princelet Street 189 men, 37 women and 64 children were listed, a total of 290 compared to 200, 30, 40 and 270 respectively at 16 Princelet Street, the only mention of such a synagogue to be found anywhere; the round figures also suggest a certain amount of 'being economical with the truth'. Total attendance throughout London was 26,612; only in the West End and St. Johns Wood synagogues did the attendance of women come anywhere near that of the men.

At the end of April sanitary works required by the borough council were completed with the aid of a £50 loan from the Federation repairs and decorations fund repayable at £10 per annum, even though difficulty was being experienced with repayment of the Society loan for the earlier refurbishment. Two special general meetings of the Society were held in May to consider the possibility of converting into a divisional society and a sub-committee was formed to effect the change. For the next biennial term of the Federation board commencing at the 30th June meeting (thirty-eight synagogues were represented for this term) five representatives were elected plus another for the Burial Society. It was at this meeting that the above £50 loan was approved. For the annual gathering this year on 13th October invitations were sent to Rabbis Chaikin and Melnick while Mrs Abrahams presented another Ark curtain. At the annual meeting on 13th December Mark Silverstone, son of the former President Philip Silverstone, was elected to that office, an office he was to hold until retirement in 1936 when he was made Life-President, dying at the age of 93 in 1963; at the subsequent Loyal United Friends Benefit Society meeting he was also elected President. To the next committee meeting it was reported that a *chevra* wished to amalgamate but it had a rabbi who was paid £1 10s. 0d. a week. Another minute from the same meeting tells us that a deputation was going to see the Chief Rabbi but neither the reason for this nor the name of the *chevra* wishing to amalgamate are recorded. Minutes of subsequent meetings record donations of various amounts to an appeal to clear the mortgage for which assistance had been obtained from Rev. Michael Adler and a promise of support from the Chief Rabbi, £20 each by Lord Rothschild and Mr Mocatta, a further ten guineas from Samuel Montague, a total of £76 15s. 0d. being obtained, this despite the account book showing regular payments of £10 towards the original loan. By the end of the year the published accounts show that the first loan of £100 for the reconstruction in 1893 had been fully repaid and also one guinea from the new loan.

The annual meeting of the Ladies' Holy Vestment Society in early February 1904 heard that 160 families had been assisted at a cost of £46. Later the same month the annual 7th Adar service was addressed by Rabbi David Kohn Zedek and Rabbi Chaikin who referred to the recent death of Rabbi Joseph Kohn Zedek, father of the former speaker. For emergency purposes it was decided at the May meeting to renew all gas fittings and carry out work on the roof and hall for a total of £4 15s. 0d. The High Holyday services were conducted by Rev. Fassenfeld assisted by Mr J. Miller, a new mantle was presented by Mr L. Masters, and Rabbi Chaikin gave the address on the intermediate Sabbath.

On Yom Kippur trouble arose with fighting in the street from noon onwards between synagogue worshippers and non-observant individuals, a report of the incident appearing in the following Friday's issue of the *Jewish Chronicle*. A club had recently been opened next door to the synagogue for 'Jewish socialists', one of a number in the neighbourhood. According to 'a well known resident in Princelet Street' the club had been established for a few months and had been a constant source of annoyance to the neighbours, on Friday nights there were rowdy functions going on late into the night and he was taking legal action to stop the nuisance. On Yom Kippur some of these 'socialists' walked about the street and even entered the synagogue premises smoking, food was being openly consumed in the club and passers-by were invited to join. There was no possible doubt that the disturbances which resulted were deliberately provoked and he condemned in the strongest terms this behaviour which was in flagrant disregard of the feelings and sensibilities of other Jews. The story from the organiser of the club was rather different; he maintained that those who wished to eat and smoke on Yom Kippur were just as entitled to do so as those who wished to refrain from these things; religious observance was a matter for the individual's choice. They were not against those who observed the religious practices and he only wished the so-called orthodox Jews would be more tolerant. He denied that club members had entered the synagogue while smoking or that rabbis had been invited to a concert in the club that day. The disturbances had actually commenced on New Year's Eve when a group of youths smashed the club's windows, the club managers then acting to prevent reprisals. The police were well aware of the unpleasantness and anticipated the situation; on the Monday in question the club was crowded and he was certain they had not caused the disturbance, theirs was the only restaurant in the district open and those who wished to eat had only the one place to go to. He regretted the fracas as he regretted all breaches of the law but it was not due to the club members. The police view was that the 'socialists' were entirely responsible for the affair, posters had been issued announcing free meals on the fast day and that they had insulted the respectable orthodox Jews. They also expressed surprise at some of the remarks of the magistrate. A total of eight people, including two juveniles, were charged with being disorderly in the streets of the Spitalfields district on the next day and were fined various amounts at Worship Street court. Rabbi Melnick spent the day at the Plotzker Shool and so was not present although I do recollect my father discussing the event.

Following this affair all seems to have returned to normal and the November committee meeting granted use of the vestry hall to the Plotzker Society for four quarterly meetings at 7s. 6d. per meeting and it was announced that the Ladies' Society was to present two chandeliers. (These were installed early February.) The annual meeting of the synagogue on 11th December refused a request from the Federation for use of the vestry hall as a reading room. There was an excess of income over expenditure of £17 and the Society meeting immediately following reported a £7 surplus, the President, Vice-president and Treasurer in both cases remaining as Mark Silverstone, Frits Falkenstein, Moses Joel, respectively, with M. Kutner and H. Goldberg as wardens; Dr G. Michael was elected medical officer to the Society.

On 12th February 1905 a memorial service was held for Frederick D. Mocatta who had died aged seventy-seven on 16th January. He had been a frequent benefactor of the synagogue and many other institutions, his library subsequently being donated to University College, London. In his address Rabbi Chaikin recalled how he was admired by all parties; all seemed to have lost a faithful and devoted friend and Israel a devoted advocate; he had come to show that man was created to love his fellow man, to be merciful, generous and patient. Once again the Ladies' Society reported that 140 families had been given help to the tune of £39 for Pesach and New Year, Mrs Adler, Mrs Jacobs and Mrs Joel being returned as President, Treasurer and Secretary, respectively, as in previous years. The usual 7th Adar service was addressed by Rabbis Melnick and David Kohn Zedek; in May Rev. Fassenfeld qualified as a *mohel* and the fact was duly advertised in the *Jewish Journal*, a Yiddish weekly of the time, but not in any of the English language papers. For the new two-year term of the Federation board only four representatives were sent.

Also in May the Society decided to reform itself as a divisional society and alter the rules accordingly sending £200 to a reserve fund, £100 for pensions and £400 to be shared between the members. The High Festivals passed off peacefully, there being no record of any disturbance this year. Perhaps adding to the joy of Simchat Torah an address was given by Rabbi Melnick presumably in some humorous vein. In November a third chandelier was fitted at a cost of £2 12s. 6d., this being accompanied by repairs to the skylight costing £4 10s. 0d. Despite its reorganisation, the Society was still apparently in some trouble and talks with the Tradesmen's Divisional Society were begun; the Sir Moses Montefiore Friendly Society also made overtures. The annual meetings of synagogue and society took place during December but perhaps the only point worth mentioning is that a collection in aid of the Russian Pogrom appeal raised £7.

Although barmitzvah celebrations were not an uncommon feature of the synagogue diary, their announcement in the *Jewish Chronicle* was, so it was an entirely unique occasion that on 13th January 1906 two such events held there on the same day were both advertised in the aforementioned journal, one boy being Abraham Cohen, the other Abram Marchinski. The sermon that day was preached by Rev. G. Sandelheim of Newcastle-upon-Tyne. The committee meeting of 27th March was told that a dangerous structure notice had been received from the District

Surveyor with a magistrate's order that the work must be carried out within fourteen days. These repairs would include work on the front chimney stack and sides of the mantlepiece of the second floor back room at a cost of £27. The required repairs were completed by the end of the following month and discussions undertaken with the District Surveyor concerning a fire escape, a subsequent estimate of £14 being obtained for such provision. The same meeting also heard that the Ladies' Society had contributed £8 to the mortgage fund and £3 3s. 6d for a chandelier. At its own annual meeting the Ladies' Society reported the distribution of £43 in monetary relief to families for the previous Pesach.

The death on 27th April of Isadore Elkan of 43 Weaver Street, Bethnal Green resulted in the synagogue receiving a bequest of £48 4s. 11d., being the residue of his estate after legacies to his daughters and grand-daughters, to Rabbi Melnick 'for learning on my behalf' and funeral and related expenses, these apparently amounting to £26 6s. 9d., had been paid. Another death, and a shock to everyone, was that of Mrs Joel in June for she was secretary of the Ladies' Society and the wife of Moses Joel, treasurer of both Synagogue and Friendly Society. Another indication of the ageing of the founders of the organisation was the retirement as Vice-president of the Society by Frits Falkenstein at the end of June for which he was to be paid £25 in lieu of a pension and as Vice-president of the synagogue at the end of July for which he was to receive a pension, effective from after the festivals. The November committee meeting was informed that repairs were to be carried out to the Ark and that £100 was to be repaid to the Society. In December came the announcement that Rev. Fassenfeld, reader for the past ten years, had been elected to the like position at the Dalston synagogue, Poets Road, a vacancy caused by the death earlier that year of Rev. J. Lesser. The annual meetings at the end of the year elected Isaac Finklestein as Vice-president of the synagogue and Mr. L. Ungar Vice-president of the Society. The synagogue had a deficit over the year of £14 due to the major repairs carried out. The Society waived £200 of the debt but in return required £50 of the remainder to be repaid within six months. Also negotiations were continuing with the Tradesmen's Divisional Society regarding amalgamation with an offer of £150 towards the reserve fund. Of the remaining funds £250 was to be divided among the members according to seniority.

Agreement to the amalgamation was finally reached in February. At the same time the Society was repaid £90 3s. 6d. making a total of £250 for the period. Meanwhile Maurice Lewandowsky was acting, gratuitously, as reader and it was decided to present Rev. Fassenfeld with a suitably inscribed vellum (cost three guineas) as a token of their appreciation of his services. This presentation took place at the end of March at the Dalston Synagogue. The 7th Adar service for this year was addressed by Rabbis Chaikin and David Kohn Zedek and two weeks later a special general meeting of the Society agreed to the proposed amalgamation with the Tradesmen's Divisional Society with £150 to be paid over, £40 to the reserve fund and not more than £15 for division each year. During May Lewandowsky was elected first reader at £1 per week; the appointment was short-lived for in August he was appointed as reader at the Higher Broughton Synagogue, Manchester. At a meeting of the Society on the 6th June the final details of the amalgamation (with the Tradesmen's Divisional Society) were announced. These were that the existing funds less £150 donated to the synagogue were to be shared among the members according to their years of membership since 1874 (minute books and other records prior to 1874 seem to have been lost by now) and arrears to the synagogue were to be deducted from the share-out. The lease was to be surrendered to the synagogue and only members of the former Society could be trustees and then only provided they retained their synagogue membership. The final formal meeting of the Society took place on 16th June. Subsequently the Society members presented Mr Lazarus Solomon with a pair of silver candlesticks in recognition of his past services.

The meeting of the synagogue committee of 28th July was informed that the incandescent lamps were to be replaced by tantalum lamps, that repairs to the leaded roof, stack pipes and gutters, Ark wall and west side party wall would cost £6 and that £17 had been received from the Ladies' Society. For the next Federation board term again four representatives, the same four as last time, were sent and, at the first meeting a loan of £50 from the repairs and redecorations fund was approved, thus leaving the synagogue £60 in debt to the fund. By this time forty-four congregations were represented at the Federation.

Mr and Mrs Isaac Finklestein presented the synagogue with yet another Sepher Torah, the ceremony on 1st September being conducted by Rev. Fassenfeld, addressed by Rabbi Chaikin and followed by the traditional *siyum*, nearly everyone present having filled in a letter. A month later the same couple presented a silk plush mantle with matching cover for the reading desk. By this time the synagogue possessed so many Scrolls that it was able to loan some for use during the High Festivals for a service at Brentford.

Another blow to the organisation came on 18th October, just sixteen months after that of his wife, with the death of Moses Joel, treasurer of the synagogue for some thirty years and chief *shomer* of the Board of Shechita, in his seventy-second year. In addition he had been Treasurer of the now defunct Loyal United Friends Friendly Society and was connected with several other institutions. His successor as synagogue Treasurer was Simon Goldberg. During November an interest-free loan of £50 was obtained from the Federation, presumably to help pay for the numerous repairs which had been carried out.

In February 1908 the committee was informed that a short list of three for the office of reader was prepared and the electric lighting was, again, to be renewed at a cost of ten guineas. The following month a fourth name was added to the list from which it was decided to offer the vacancy to Mr I. Silverman who, however, failed to obtain the Chief Rabbi's certificate and the post was eventually taken by Rev. M. Kay. It was also decided to charge members one shilling per quarter for seats between Ark and Bimah and sixpence for those behind. The Ladies' Society at its annual meeting in May heard that £40 had been shared among two hundred poor families during the past year. Mrs Adler had decided to retire and was succeeded as President by Mrs J. Jacobs with Mrs E. Silverstone as Vice-president and Mrs E. Berkovsky Treasurer. According to a minute of the synagogue meeting of 23rd August, flap seats were to be provided in front of the ladies' gallery for the wives of the honorary officers. I can only presume that this was an unfortunate misreading of the secretary's notes, not spotted by any of the committee members and should have read that flaps for those seats were to be provided (as book rests). The synagogue annual meeting at the end of December decided to raise weekly seat rentals to 6½d., from 1st January, elected Mr S. Rabinovits as Vice-president and was informed that the beadle, Mr Miller, had given three months notice of leaving.

In January 1909 it was announced that the Ozerkova Chevra from 18 Booth Street had amalgamated bringing two Sifrei Torah, each with silver breastplate, pointer and bells; a spice box and silver cup. The annual 7th Adar service was addressed this year, once again, by Rabbis Chaikin and David Kohn Zedek. During the year a bequest of £22 10s. 0d. from the executors of the late David Lawrence was received. A most unusual event took place on 12th February 1910 when an eight-year-old boy, Hyman Godrath, read the entire *sedra* and recited the Haphtorah. An announcement in the *Jewish Chronicle* the following Friday expressed the appreciation of the President and Wardens and also thanked his teacher Mr J. Meller.

The death in May of the King evoked widespread sorrow among the East End Jews even to the extent of raising a memorial to him opposite the

London Hospital, but reporting of the memorial services was somewhat scant and we only read in both the *Jewish Chronicle* and *Jewish World* that the Rev. M. Kay conducted the service at Princes Street, there being no further detail, not even of the speaker. On 22nd January the next year, a memorial service was held, this time for Lord Swaythling (Samuel Montague), founder of the Federation, when the report was the reverse, naming the speaker, Rabbi Melnick, but not the reader. For the nostalgic 18th February was an important Shabbat owing to a visit by Rev. Fassenfeld who conducted the service, Rev. Kay having decided to leave. He was eventually succeeded by Jacob Glowitch. On 27th August the final link with the founders was broken when Jane, widow of the late Coleman Angel, passed away in her eighty-second year. Meanwhile the synagogue itself was redecorated in time for the New Year services led by Rev. Glowitch assisted by Mr D. Strauss.

The year 1912 seems to have been of little interest to the press. Nevertheless it is recorded that the Chevra Tehillim had a surplus of £14 over the year, its total funds were now £654 and membership 313. The usefulness of the building to the community might be judged by its use by five separate societies at mid-May in addition to the Chevra Tehillim, each paying a fee for a room for its meetings. The Federation set up a fund in memory of Lord Swaythling to which Princelet Street Synagogue contributed £10 18s. 0d. By the end of the year all repayment of the loans were completed and no further loans from any Federation funds are recorded.

At the synagogue annual meeting on 19th January 1913 we read among the appointments that of M. Reback as collector. That this was of particular significance was that Myer Reback who had actually commenced duties during the previous April remained officially as collector until his death at the age of eighty-four in December 1961, often acting as assistant reader, and was the regular reader of the Sedra, his son Simon later becoming secretary and a widowed daughter taking on the role of caretaker, enabling services to be held during winter afternoons after the official closure right up until the sale in 1980. The same year also seems to have seen the resignation of Rev. Glowitch as reader, his place being taken early the following year by Mark Goldfine although the report of the annual general meeting at the end of December does not mention the election of a reader and I have found no mention of the new reader until December 1918 when both the *Jewish Chronicle* and *Jewish World* included his name as having helped collect sums of money for the Zionist Preparation Fund at the Princelet Street Synagogue.

With the coming of the Great War the emphasis of the Jewish press turned from largely parochial matters to more worldly ones and the activities of the various organisations rapidly became less well reported. Indeed the few reports concerning Princelet Street Synagogue were mainly concerned with collections for various charities but there were a number of barmitzvah announcements during the period, one stating that there were to be no festivities as the boy's father was detained in Russian Poland. Another unusual announcement also during 1915 was that of the marriage of a couple both of whom had been inmates of the Home for Aged Jews at Wandsworth Common.

One of the consequences of the conflict was the ending of the Ottoman Empire in the Middle East including the conquest of Palestine by the British army. With this came the Balfour declaration dated 2nd November 1917 which stated that 'His Majesty's Government view with favour the establishment of a national home for the Jewish people in Palestine,' this only twenty years after the first Zionist Congress. The synagogue was represented at, and sent a message of support to, a 'Great Thanksgiving Meeting' at the London Opera House on Sunday 2nd December, the meeting being chaired by Lord Rothschild to whom the declaration had been addressed. This spurred numerous speakers and meetings in support of the Zionist Organisation generally with fund raising in mind and the Princelet Street Synagogue hosted its fair share of them. As a result of these meetings considerable sums of money were raised in support of the settlements being established in the Holy land.

Chapter 8

The Synagogue in the Mid-Twentieth Century

Rab. Helbo, quoting Rab. Huna said: One should not leave the house of G-d with hurried footsteps.

(Talmud Berakhoth 6b)

By the end of the first world war Princelet Street had long lost its dominance as the principal synagogue in Spitalfields, this role having been taken by the Spitalfields Great Synagogue, better known as the Machzike Hadass almost from its inception, close by on the corner of Brick Lane and Fournier Street. It was very much larger and offered anyone wishing to say a *kaddish* or recite his prayers for whatever reason, *minyan* at any time of the day, there being groups of people studying on the premises at all times. Yet, having been opened with some assistance from Princelet Street, it was outlived by some six years although with considerable difficulty. Indeed Princelet Street was the first in Spitalfields to open its doors, the last to close them; its ghost still lives on, The Machzike Hadass community still lives on but it is only a vestige of its former glory and is no longer in the East End.

The departure of Rabbi Melnick just before Pesach 1920 for the newly opened Commercial Road Great Synagogue brought an end to an era for he had been there for almost a quarter of a century, technically as the rabbi of the Chevra Tehillim but then generally recognised as synagogue rabbi. Despite this he was never employed on a full time basis for in addition to being a *shochet* for the Shechita Board he was also at various times *rav* of the Old Castle Street and the Plotzker Synagogues and frequently assisted others at times when one might have expected him to be in Princelet Street. He had joined the organisation on the death of Rabbi Cohen, first rabbi of the Chevra Tehillim, in 1896. His successor, Rabbi Davidson, was employed by both synagogue and Chevra Tehillim, synagogue paying him an additional five shillings a week. Even so he was still on part time terms.

Once again, in 1921 the synagogue underwent refurbishment and was reopened and reconsecrated on Sunday 17th April that year by Sir Stuart Samuel and Dayan Feldman respectively, service being conducted by Rev. Goldfine assisted by the choir of the Great Synagogue under the direction of Samuel Alman. In his homily the *dayan* pointed out that this was the second occasion on which the synagogue had undergone extensive renovation; compared this event with the erection of the tabernacle in the wilderness having taken place in the same Hebrew month and, indeed, on the same Hebrew date as the previous reopening twenty-eight years earlier. He trusted that it would be retained as a house of study and charity as well as a house of prayer as it had been in its earlier years. Dayan Chaikin also addressed the gathering in Yiddish. A month later Mark Moses, President of the Chevra Tehillim, by now living at Stamford Hill, died in his sixty-seventh year.

In September another Sepher Torah was presented, replete with silver crown, breastplate and pointer, by Mr & Mrs I. Zimmerman to mark their silver wedding. Offerings made at this function totalled £8 2s. 0d. It appears that to control the expected attendance at this function a police presence was considered advisable and this cost 15 shillings.

Another important event of the year was the retirement of Isaac Kaliski as secretary of Princelet Street Synagogue, a post he had occupied since 1893, and the Chevra Tehillim for even longer, and was presented with a framed, illuminated address. He was succeeded as synagogue secretary by Mr J. M. Passer and as Chevra Tehillim secretary by Mr. H Kintzler. (In December the following year Kaliski was convicted on season ticket offences and subsequently resigned all public offices.) Kaliski died 5th March 1934.

In response to a request from the secretary Lady Rothschild sent a £5 donation towards the floral decorations for Shavuot. That this was more than sufficient is indicated by the account book entries which show the cost never to have exceeded £3 and part of this was offset by sales after the festival. This became an annual donation continuing until 1934. The United Synagogue interest in the building was maintained when during the year its welfare committee opened a free advisory centre in the premises. Also during the year Booth Street, continuous with Princelet

Street East of Brick Lane, was incorporated into Princelet Street and numbering rearranged to the more conventional system with odd numbers one side, evens the other. Thus 18 became 19. In January 1925 Rev. John Harris replaced Rev. Hirsch although there appears to have been a hiatus between the two appointments. The centre remained at the premises until May 1928 when it was transferred to 22 Buxton Street. Also Rabbi Davidson left on 14th December.

The major event of 1924 was the election of a representative, Mr I. K. Morris, to the Board of Deputies, his first attendance being on the 19th January that year. Rabbi Schwartz was appointed to succeed Rabbi Davidson in March and in November the synagogue increased its subvention to his salary by 50%. In early September Sarah Goldfine, wife of the *chazan*, died, the funeral taking place on the 10th. A collection to defray the cost of a new *paroches* was started and the article made and installed at a cost of £11 8s. 8d. early the following year. The United Synagogue Welfare Committee's advisory centre at the synagogue was reopened during February with Rev. John S. Harris in attendance. On 18th February Rev. Goldfine married Golda Levy, Dayan Hillman and Rev. Signiewsky being the celebrants. Rev. Goldfine was presented with a pair of candlesticks and a cheque for fifteen guineas of which one-third came from synagogue funds, the remainder from the members. During July Abraham Moses, one of the founder members of the Chevra Tehillim, died aged seventy-five. He had held various other communal positions including that of trustee of the Mile End New Town Synagogue which he had assisted in founding.

The silver jubilee of Mark Silverstone's presidency occurred in 1926 when he was presented at a reception at Monnickendam's restaurant in Aldersgate Street with a silver candelabra. Agreement was reached with Stepney Borough Council to fix brass sockets into the pavement outside the doorway so that an awning could be erected for weddings. The support fittings above the door are still present. On 16th December 1927 Marks and Rosetta Gumpright celebrated their golden wedding. This is the earliest couple married in the synagogue under the cheap marriages (see Chapter 5) arrangement that I have been able to find.

Problems with the house roof were a regular feature of the calendar and during 1928 it was decided to replace the existing structure, architect being J. Warwick Betteridge and builder N. Lipshak, total cost £107 7s. 0d. In December Rabbi Schwartz resigned. The United Synagogue Welfare Committee's centre moved away to new, more convenient premises in Buxton Street, off Brick Lane opened by the Chief Rabbi during May. In early February Rabbi Weinstein, followed the next week by Rabbi Woolf, preached, the former being awarded the vacant post at a salary of £4 per week of which the Chevra Tehillim contributed £3 12s. 6d. In July the synagogue increased his salary by fifteen shillings.

During January 1930 the Chevra Tehillim's contribution towards the Rabbi's salary was reduced to £2 17s. 6d., cutting his emoluments to £4 per week and in September they stopped contributing totally so that from then he received only £1 2s. 6d. This was probably not as bad as it may seem since he was also a *shochet*. Also, the precise position of the Chevra Tehillim's contribution to the rabbi's salary remains unclear since the annual statement of accounts for the year November 1938-1939 (one of the only two balance sheets of the Chevra Tehillim still extant) shows an item of expenditure for rabbi's salary of £45 10s. 0d. (17s. 6d. per week) for both that and the previous years, suggesting that although the contribution was reduced, what was left was paid directly.

During 1931 two series of leaflets were prepared, one announcing the abolition of offerings, the other asking ladies to come forward to join and assist the Ladies' Society. In January 1933 salaries of reader, rabbi and collector were reduced by 10s., 5s. and 2s. 6d. respectively although the gratuities they received for the High Festivals were not affected.

Although it had been the policy of the various community organisations to persuade people to move out of the East End, by 1934 the policy was really beginning to bite among the more recent arrivals as we see that Princelet Street, having had to reduce staff salaries, was now having to employ a *minyan* man from the beginning of this year, presumably for the weekday services, at 2s. 6d. per week. In November a second *minyan* man was taken on. The £5 donation from Lady Rothschild this year appears to have been the last.

The two *minyan* men each received a gratuity of eight shillings for Pesach 1935. In time for the festival a number of minor repairs and redecorations were carried out and at the end of the year Mr A. Marks, who had been Baal Shacharis for many years, left. There was no apparent replacement and it must be assumed that Myer Reback assumed the office although his remuneration did not increase.

On 28th January 1936 Yetta Leah, widow of Philip Silverstone, second President of both synagogue and Society, died. She had outlived her husband by almost thirty-six years and her son Mark was on the point of retiring as the fourth president which he did at the Annual General meeting in February. He was succeeded by Dr Mark Louis Barst and was elected life president. Another death, on 19th January, was that of Mrs

Elizabeth Taylor Meredith, who had inherited the freehold of the property from her father Henry Bawtree and it now became vested in that of her husband, Lawrence Bawtree Meredith. The Baal Shacharis for the 1937 High Festivals was J. Malinsky who was paid £10 for his efforts.

The lease granted in 1889 was due to expire 29th September 1939 but the contemporary freeholder granted a new lease to Mark Louis Barst of 16 Wilkes Street, Spitalfields (President of the synagogue) and Louis Levy of 59 Bethune Road, Stoke Newington, both trustees, for a term of 49 years from 24th June. It was similar to the earlier lease but contained an additional clause placing upon the leasees an obligation 'during such period as this country may be engaged in war with any foreign state to keep insured the demised premises against destruction or damage by shots shells bombs or missiles projected from or used against aerial craft or by bombardment of hostile guns.' There was also a clause allowing the leasees in certain circumstances to purchase the freehold. Solicitor's fees and incidentals were in excess of £20 paid in two instalments.

The following year, Nancy, daughter of Myer Reback, married and was given £5 as a present. By June the financial position had worsened with now at least two quarters each year showing a deficit, so that the salaries of reader, rabbi and collector were reduced to £3, £1 13s. 0d. and 15s. respectively while the quarterly payment to the secretary went down to £6. However the rabbi was paid an extra 4d. per week on behalf of the burial society.

The outbreak of war in September 1939 necessitated a total blackout for which six yards of suitable material were purchased to cover the windows and the skylight was obscured with blackout paper.

In January, J. Warwick Betteridge, Architects were paid a 5 guinea fee and subsequently Wilson & Moore, builders, £94 7s. 0d. In June the same architect received 14 guineas concerning roof repairs and the builders £11 15s. 0d. There is a further entry in the accounts of eleven shillings to the builder in December. What the precise linkage between these entries is I do not know. During March £500 was transferred from the bank to be invested in 3% defence bonds. The Annual statement of the Chevra Tehillim for its AGM on 10th March 1940, already referred to, showed a further fall in membership to 108 and a deficit on current account of £18 11s. 10d. compared with almost £29 the previous year. This is the last record I have found of the Chevra Tehillim. A mysterious entry appears in the accounts for 12th November. The architect named above was paid a 10 guinea fee concerning a report on the Poltava Synagogue. (Assuming this was the one in Spital Square which had been bombed it may have been a report on whether the structure could be saved.) To my mind this could only mean that an amalgamation was being contemplated. The building suffered some damage during the Battle of Britain/Blitz and repairs costing £13 8*s.* 0*d.* were carried out during the early months of 1941; in May ten Siphrei Torah and two *megillot* were transferred to Rev. Goldfine's safe keeping in Croydon while Dr Barst sheltered two large scrolls and Joseph Kalman one small one. In August amalgamation with the Wilkes Street Synagogue, after protracted negotiations which appear to have started in late 1937, was achieved; an advertisement to that effect appearing in the Yiddish newspaper *Die Zeit* in September. The redundant seating appears to have been sold to the Philpot Street Synagogue which had been destroyed in an air raid and was now housed in temporary premises. A Mr I. Goldstein of Wilkes Street Synagogue received £140 in two instalments and the secretary's salary was increased to £10 per quarter on account of the extra work involved.

During January 1942 the War Damage Commission paid £30 14*s.* 9*d.* in compensation although a note by the item says that £31 11*s.* 0*d.* had actually been spent. For the High Holydays Myer Reback replaced Mr Malinsky as Baal Shacharis for which he was paid £7 while the displaced Malinsky received £5 in compensation. Also at the end of the year the salaries of both rabbi and reader were increased by 4*s.* 8*d.* a week paid quarterly at £3. Some property was stored by Davis, Turner & Co. from October at £1 7*s.* 0*d.* a quarter, presumably some of the furniture from Wilkes Street.

Mr S. Berg, a warden and president of the Chevra Tehillim and former synagogue vice-president, died at the end of April 1943, tombstone being consecrated during November of the following year. An entry in the account book records £130 being raised by the sale of six *sephorim* from 32 Dunk Street. In August, Sarah, daughter of Rabbi Weinstein, married and was given a five guinea wedding present. A month later the rabbi resigned to take up the post of Rosh Hashochetim. I understand that with falling membership there was some encouragement from the committee. Mr Malinsky again received £5 in lieu while Myer Reback assisted the *chazan* during the High Festivals and in October Samuel Postansky succeeded Rabbi Weinstein but left the following January. The father of Dr Barst the President, also a member, died at the end of the following January. In April David Deutsch filled the ministerial vacancy but stayed only till mid-June. August saw the reimbursement by the War Damage Commission of £51 12*s.* 6*d.* for expenses incurred. Rev. Shlomo Halstuck was next to fill the ministerial vacancy from February 1945. In November the Reader's salary was increased by £1 a week. Rev. Halstuk left in February 1946 about the same time as an advertisement in *Die Zeit* for a new part-time secretary. The notice appeared on six successive days and was in English. Mr Passer left at the end of March when the highly detailed entries in the account book ceased and only brief quarterly summaries were provided. It appears that he was succeeded by Mr S. Kushner.

Following an instruction from the Stepney Borough Council the next year the area surrounds and gratings in front of the house, which were in a defective condition and a danger to pedestrians, were repaired. During January 1948, Kushner, the secretary, was paid £14 6s. 5d. in full settlement of salary in lieu of notice. Chazan Mark Goldfine was given a £250 gratuity to mark his long service to the Shool. This payment was ruled as assessable by the income tax authority. The cheque was subsequently returned. There was long correspondence over this and it was eventually paid, some intervention by the Beth Din having taken place. There does not appear to be any further information over the tax position.

An entry of £3 2s. 6d. for a party for Shavuot 1949 suggests that the Chevra Tehillim had disbanded but that its annual Shavuot celebration was being continued. Simon Reback (son of Myer) was appointed marriage secretary from 9th May.

Dr Barst tendered his resignation as President in September 1950 on the grounds of ill health but was persuaded to stay on. Mark Goldfine resigned as reader after thirty-seven years service but continued as minister to the Federation. He was succeeded by Noach Kaplin. It appears that Rev. Halstuck was asked to act in an honorary capacity but was prepared to accept only on the condition that he was given full status as official minister of religion. One item of interest this year was that the compensation payment for being called to the reading of the *tochecho* was raised to 5s. from 2s. 6d., a level it had been since its first days. Mr I. Zimmerman wrote to the secretary during November about a Sepher Torah, mantle and set of silver, presumably the ones he had presented in 1921 on his silver wedding.

To mark his forty years' service to the congregation as collector and second reader Myer Reback was presented with an illuminated address and a substantial sum of money in appreciation of his services by Dr Barst, the President, who retired as from 1st December 1951 and was succeeded by Mr J. Goldstein. Dr. Barst died on December 20th 1954.

As a result of the death of Lawrence Bawtree Meredith on 7th November, the property passed to his second wife Olive Clara who took an active interest in the condition of the building despite living in Sanderstead,

Surrey. In a letter dated July 1953 she asked for details of when the premises were last decorated as she had passed by recently and considered that they were in need of repair. (The lease required painting every fourth year.) A response detailed recent repairs and a subsequent letter from her said that she would give notice when she wanted to inspect the interior.

Plans were laid for amalgamation with the Mile End New Town Synagogue, Dunk Street but the marriage was never consummated. A facsimile of the leaflet dated March 1952 detailing the proposed changes is shown at appendix v. The scheme for the proposed merger indicated that there was a difference in weekly subscription between the two congregations which was to be preserved as were all the rights of the members of both congregations All the assets were to become those of Princelet Street and the two existing sets of Honorary Officers were to be retained for twelve months following the merger after which a single set of Hon. Officers and one committee would be elected. Mile End New Town appeared to have only a beadle and collector as paid staff, of which the beadle was already in receipt of a pension and the collector's services would be required for only a further twelve months, while Princelet Street had a secretary who was to be retired under the scheme, and a collector/beadle and a reader, both of whom would be retained. The major change here was to be that 'No paid official shall be called upon to retire annually'. During January a silver Chanuka *menorah* for £12 10s. 0d. and in July old chandeliers for £1 17s. 6d. were sold. In May the bank wrote to the President, complaining that letters sent to 19 Princelet Street were being returned marked 'Gone Away'.

From the end of the second quarter 1955 no summaries or audits of accounts appear in the books.

Rev. Kaplin wrote to the secretary in August 1957 asking for his salary to be raised to the level promised after six months service as he was still receiving only the same as when he had started; he had also not received the customary Pesach gift this year. Any reply was clearly negative and he resigned in early September. Among the archives is a draft of a letter expressing surprise at the resignation and threatening to take the matter to the Beth Din. A new reader was appointed at below Rev. Kaplin's salary but it also necessitated taking on a Baal Musaph for the High Festivals. Olive Meredith died on 30th October, the property now being bequeathed to her son (or step-son) Frank of Tottenham.

During June 1958 a Sepher Torah was sold for £75 and another the following January for £70; the next February the new reader's salary was reduced by 10s. a week.

On 27th December 1961 Myer Reback died, having given a half century of service to the synagogue in various capacities. 22nd November 1962 saw the passing of Mark Silverstone in his ninety-third year, his wife dying the following 4th February in her eighty-eighth year. He left estate of £2,017 (£1,873 net). The couple had been married at Dukes Place Synagogue on 6th March 1895 by Chief Rabbi Hermann Adler, Revs. Hast and Gordon.

The last entry in the account book was for 26th February 1962 and showed total income for the year ending 28th February as £778 5s. 6d. and expenditure £802 9s. 1d., both figures including an item of £2 16s. 6d. for the Joint Palestine Appeal.

The synagogue officers faced with the, by now, impossibility of obtaining a *minyan* for its Shabbat services decided to accept the inevitable and abandoned the building, leaving behind the second floor flat occupied by a widowed daughter of Myer Reback acting as caretaker, and the garret flat occupied by David Rodinsky, a recluse, who left one day in late 1969 not to return. (He collapsed in the street and died a few days later in hospital aged forty-nine.) During the winter, afternoon services were held at lunch times for people working in the district, first in the synagogue itself but later as the condition of the roof deteriorated and rain poured in, in the ground floor front room which was also used as a classroom by the nearby Etz Chaim Yeshiva.

During 1970 the synagogue formally amalgamated with Bethnal Green Great Synagogue. Nevertheless a separate membership section for Princelet Street members was maintained. The winter *mincha* services also continued.

In 1980 the Federation of Synagogues exercised the option in the lease to buy the freehold of the building at a cost of £35,000 and subsequently sold it to the Spitalfields Historic Buildings Trust at the same price. The widow who had looked after the building for so many years was rehoused by the council. Thus, this historic building, having been passed down the family for 277 years, was sold twice within a period of months. The remaining scrolls were removed by the Federation together with some of the more important books but many were left behind, together with some of the fabrics scattered about as though the Shool had been abandoned in some sudden emergency. Much of this material was further damaged by rain and dust from the disintegrating plasterwork. These were removed to a store of the Museum of London where they were allowed to dry out in an unheated store for a number of years before they could be examined. Emergency repairs were carried out to roof and windows to weatherproof and the interior made safe; the Heritage Centre was set up under its own committee to raise funds in order to restore the house to its original condition for use as a museum to its past and a resource centre for the current immigrant community of the district.

Chapter 9

A Review of a Century of the Princelet Street Synagogue

Remember the days of old. Consider the years of many generations; ask your father and he will show you, your elders and they will tell you.
(Deuteronomy XXXII 7)

Having read some details of the history of the Princelet Street Synagogue one can now look back and ask, and perhaps conjecture, on its *raison d'être*. In the mid-nineteenth century there was no national welfare provision of any sort. Poverty at this time reigned supreme, a symptom of it being the workhouse. A working week could be eighty hours long with little time for breaks of any kind; many even ate and slept at their work benches. Wages were meagre and should workers be absent for any reason, whether sick or for another problem, they were not paid. For the sick there was, in addition, the problem of paying for medical attention, for medicines and hospital care. Financing of retirement was another problem and many worked on until no longer able. To overcome these problems, groups of people would form mutual benefit or friendly societies which collected a fee of a few pence (perhaps only one or two) each week and, in return, paid out sickness and unemployment benefit, medical charges, hospital fees, burial and tombstone costs. Some of these societies employed a doctor for their members. In the Jewish community these were usually associated with a synagogue, which also paid a benefit during the *shiva* week. The fee may have been wholly or partly included in the synagogue membership fee. The usual practice was for a group of working people to get together to form a congregation and obtain premises in a room converted for the purpose, or even just modified from its normal

111

workaday use. The necessary appurtenances for worship would be obtained and they would then set up its welfare or friendly society.

The origins of the Princelet Street Shool were, perhaps, the reverse of the norm. The founding fathers of the Loyal United Friends Friendly Society were themselves employers of labour, being small business men. The Society was set up in 1862 specifically to assist fellow Jews, largely recent arrivals, living in the Spitalfields area, in regard to the problems outlined above. For these immigrants the problems, bad enough for the native population, must have been magnified several times. Not only was it difficult for them to get jobs of any sort, but the fact that they could not speak English left them open to exploitation of many forms. Although the society founders had come from Eastern Europe, they had been in England for many years and become accustomed to the general ways of the settled Anglo-Jewish community except that their religious observance was on a considerably higher plane. They also saw a need for a place of worship in the Spitalfields area, there being none east of Sandys Row, which catered primarily for those of Dutch origin, or north of Prescott Street, itself very small. Yet in Spitalfields there was a growing Jewish population owing to the steady trickle of mainly poor immigrants from Poland, Lithuania and other parts of the Russian empire.

The Society members obtained rooms in a house in Fashion Street and held regular services, usually well-attended. By 1865 pressure on the space was such that it was not possible to hold the High Festival services there and a hall in Leadenhall Street was hired for the period. At this time the status of the worshipping group was regularised and for a small additional fee Society members also became synagogue members, membership of one being conditional upon membership of the other. Both membership and attendances were becoming too great for the Fashion Street rooms and new premises had to be found. Larger rooms in the area were no answer to the problem since few were available and in any case were not much larger.

In late 1869 Jacob Davidson, President of both Society and congregation and owner of a boot and shoe warehouse at 15/16 Princes Street (23/25), learned that number 18 was vacant and that the landlord was seeking a long term tenant. This was a four storey house with a basement and a workshop at the rear still leaving a significant garden. The idea put forward was that the workshop be demolished, the garden excavated and a suitable building erected. The Bawtree family who were the landlords granted a twenty-year lease and with their permission the alterations went ahead, the final product incorporating parts of the house into the prayer hall, some as a permanent feature, some only when required. The design, which was based on that of the New Synagogue in Great St. Helens, has already been described. From the opening, the management of synagogue and Society were separate entities although the personnel were almost entirely the same.

The cost of the building was about £1,100 of which the existing membership contributed £600 and the remainder was raised by public appeal. That the membership at that time could raise so much was in itself remarkable since this was one of the poorest areas of Jewish settlement in London. With a membership little over a hundred it means that each donated an average of about £6, an exceedingly large sum considering that an artisan then would consider himself very well paid at £1 a week. Even more remarkable was that the remaining £500 was raised by outside contributions following only two successive appeal advertisements in the press and with no subsequent lists of donors and their donations as was the practice of the period. From the start a regular reader was employed but no rabbi, sermons were preached by various visiting rabbis and even United Synagogue ministers. It soon became of major importance as both synagogue and general meeting place and the Jewish Association for the Diffusion of Religious Knowledge eventually made it one of their principal bases. A succession of readers is reported, generally remaining until well established and then leaving for better paid posts, some within the United Synagogue.

The second society, the Chevra Tehillim, founded in 1873, did not employ a permanent rabbi until 1882 when Rabbi Louis Cohen was appointed and was succeeded on his death in 1895 by Rabbi Melnick. Both were generally recognised as rabbi of the synagogue, attending regularly, acting as its religious authority, preaching whenever considered reasonable, occasionally being paid extra by the synagogue for their trouble, and being fully involved in the congregational activities. Also, when necessary both assisted with the conducting of the services, all this despite concurrently holding positions as rabbi of other synagogues. The Shool itself did not contribute to the rabbis' wages until after the departure of Rabbi Melnick in 1920. Even then it was a small subvention until the early 1930s when the situation was reversed with the Shool paying the greater part. Eventually the two organisations paid the incumbent separately. Prayer in the synagogue was of the somewhat informal framework, typical of eastern Europe rather than the formality of the English style as embodied in the United Synagogue. Sermons were usually given in Yiddish or German, more rarely in English.

Synagogue finance was always a problem. Almost all the members were artisans of some description and poorly paid, few had their own business. Weekly subscription was about sixpence and membership rarely exceeded two hundred and for much of the time was less than half that. Many could not even afford that amount. For several years, from 1924, Lady Rothschild gave a £5 donation for the Shavuot floral decorations, the cost of which amounted only to some £2, nearly half being retrieved by their subsequent sale. The photograph taken in the early years of this century indicates that generally potted plants were used and the positioning of nails (recently removed) along the base of the gallery walls supports this so that good quality plants were obtained by the buyers.

Moral matters were also a consideration for the officers; one man had his membership withdrawn after it became known that he had been associating with a woman other than his wife who, as a result, had given birth to a child. However it appears that his membership was restored some time later.

One continuing problem was the state of the house roof. This was constructed of two parallel ridges with a valley between, all being parallel to the house frontage, therefore not visible from the street. Drainage of this was through a collecting trough and stack pipe, the system being adequate so long as the trough was kept clear. Unfortunately access was difficult and various forms of detritus including dead birds, especially pigeons, accumulated to block the rain water egress, causing flooding and damage to both roof and the ceilings immediately below. In an attempt to overcome the problem at one time the original pantiles had been replaced with slates but to little avail. During 1928 and again, as part of the restoration work during 1990, the entire house roof was replaced, this second time using the original pantile type covering but also with modern style underfelt and with precautions against the dead birds and other detritus.

The membership of the Shool waxed and waned from time to time but it seems never to have made any significant gains from the post-1881 immigration surge although, it seems, it was always well attended and attracted good *chazanim* and *rabbanim*. Even the presence of the Machzike Hadass (Spitalfields Great Synagogue) just around the corner does not seem to have reduced attendances significantly, at least until near the beginning of the second World War. From then on decline set in rapidly and the move away from the area, accelerated by that war, put the finishing touches to it. Although it was, probably, the last in Spitalfields 'to die' its passing was long and painful. Many a Shabbat morning someone would be standing outside to catch a passer-by to make the essential *minyan*. For weekday services this became routine.

Although marriages were a regular feature of the synagogue there were, in total, fewer than 400 between 1897 and 1955 when the last took place. In an attempt to encourage more, an entrance canopy was erected during 1926 but with little success. As indicated, the synagogue was the main place for the cheap marriage scheme of the United Synagogue from 1877 to 1890, when they were transferred to the East London in Rectory Square. It has not been possible to determine the actual number that took place during that period although I do possess documents and other evidence of a few of these.

Especially in its early days it was the only synagogue in the area able to boast both a hall and a room for meetings so that both were in frequent use for a wide variety of purposes including social functions such as weddings and barmitzvahs. One of the earliest meetings which took place here was on 19th February 1871 for the purpose of forming a 'Society for Promoting a Jewish Workhouse'. Owing to a poor attendance it was adjourned to 10th March when the attendance was too large for the available seating. As a result a workhouse was established at 123 Wentworth Street, subsequently moved to 37/39 Stepney Green, then amalgamated with the much older Hand-in-Hand Society and Widows' Home Asylum to form the Home for Aged Jews, now at Nightingale House, Wandsworth.

It appears that the level of religious observance of the members varied fairly widely and this could be judged by their behaviour. An elderly gentleman informs me that in about 1920 an older cousin of his described the situation:

> The men who wore very big *tallesim* with black stripes were much more pious than those who wore medium sized blue and white *tallesim*; those who swayed back and forth (*shockled*) at 10 per minute were more pious than those who *shockled* at only 3 per minute and those who swayed from side to side were even more pious than the others.

Another item of recollection by my informant above was of the preachers. The Shool would be crowded to hear the words of wisdom preached by the *maggid*, who may well have been my grandfather, with a good sprinkling of ladies in the gallery above. My informant's knowledge of Yiddish was insufficient to cope with the homily and he was rarely if ever able to follow the argument. After some time one of the women above would start sobbing and this, like yawning, being infectious, soon had the rest of the gallery joining in. At this point the *shammas* would bang on the desk and call for silence. During an oration lasting an hour or two or, perhaps, even longer, this event might recur on several occasions. He was not sure whether the *maggid* considered this happening a sign of the success of the sermon.

The following costings for the annual gathering in October 1930 might be of interest to the reader:

75 couples @ 8*s*.	£30
13 whisky @ 12*s*.	£7 16*s*. 0*d*.
2 cherry brandy @ 11*s*.	£1 2*s*. 0*d*.
2 wine @ 3*s*. 9*d*.	7*s*. 6*d*.

The annual gathering was, of course, the Simchat Torah party but this appears to have been the only one with the costings spelt out in this detail although regular purchases of wine for *kiddush* and *havdalah* are recorded. The other annual gathering was of the Chevra Tehillim on Shavuot which appears to have been taken over by the Shool following the collapse of the Chevra during the war. No details of its costings have been found.

In a letter from Mr J.M. Passer, secretary, to the secretary of the Federation of Synagogues dated 26th January 1939, it is suggested that a history of the Princelet Street Synagogue could be prepared for the Federation's Jubilee Report. This would date back to its foundation in 1862 but would be time-consuming as reference would have to be made to the various people, solicitors and others and the committee would be prepared to put all records at the disposal of the Federation if it would undertake to do the work. Mr Jung replied that he would be happy to go through all the documents if he could be allowed sight of them for a while. Since the Jubilee of the Federation occurred more than a year prior to this correspondence it seems rather late to start such a report. In any case no such document seems to have come into existence and the only record of the Federation Jubilee appears to have been a book written by Dr Cecil Roth and published without his permission.

Following the war the declining attendances received a slight boost with the closing of the Spitalfields Great in 1957 but this was short lived. Most of the members moved away east to Ilford or to the north-west suburbs, many transferring membership to more local Federation synagogues although membership lists among the archives indicate a significant number who did not. However, the loss of income was not sustainable and, together with poor attendances, closure was inevitable.

One might have thought that closing the synagogue would have been an orderly process with all items either removed or stored away in suitable containers. True the Siphrei Torah and some of the more valuable books were removed by the Federation of Synagogues staff but other items were left scattered about, Ark curtain and desk coverings left *in situ*. General deterioration between the closure and the sale in 1980 resulted in severe damage to the material left behind in the synagogue itself although books, etc. which were in the front room merely gathered dust. Of most interest among this archive was, what appears to have been, the entire collection of white Torah mantles, one being decorated entirely with pearls.

Many donations going back to the re-opening in 1893 are recorded on the facias of the ladies' gallery. These include the donations for that appeal from the Chief Rabbi of the time, the Rothschilds, Samuel Montague and even the freeholder. Some give the Hebrew name only and so it is almost impossible now to identify the donor, others give both Hebrew and English names. Some of the more recent inscriptions have errors with one showing the name of the Hebrew month mis-spelt and the date forty-four years later than the event commemorated. That is not to say that all the English spellings are correct.

Alexander Tertis appears to have remarried; he died 25th June 1918 leaving a wife, sons and daughters. His youngest daughter was engaged to Maurice Halter of Liverpool on 4th July 1902. Philip Fassenfeld died in 1938 and was buried at Plashet; his wife and a daughter were interred alongside.

Appendix i

A Humble *Chevra* Room

It is well known that much of the early period described in this book was one of great poverty with many having just the bare means of existence but just how bad things were for some is borne out by the following article which appeared in the *Jewish Chronicle* of 23rd August 1895 under the title of 'A Humble Chevra Room' the Author being 'A Visitor Among the Poor' and which I reproduce without comment.

> I often think that if visitors among the Jewish poor were to relate the experiences they come across in the course of their philanthropic labours, they might furnish now and again some interesting reading to the outside public who have a very vague idea of how our foreign poor live, move and have their being. Not very long ago I encountered an experience so novel that I feel sure your readers will be interested in what I have to say. I went to visit a woman who was lying ill at a certain house in Hanbury Street whose occupants are not unknown to the Jewish Board of Guardians. Bikur Cholim is the term usually applied to this *mitzvah* on which I was intent. I made my way up a pair of rather steep and winding stairs which led into a room. Let me try and describe the room. It was rather large for the neighbourhood and was a sort of kitchen. It had an ample fireplace the top of which formed an open recess in which a number of all sorts of objects could be stowed away. By the side of this fireplace was a kitchen dresser with its ordinary supply of cups and saucers and crockery. A long table and forms made of the roughest deal and put together in an amateurish, not to say clumsy way, formed other items of furniture. The room led into a bedroom and there were large windows in the partitioning wall so that they could see into the bedroom even when the door was shut, quite easily. Another flight of stairs led from the room to the apartments above.
>
> The woman I had come to see had had an accident. She had fallen down the stairs which led into the street and was lying in bed in the large kitchen I have described. Well, there was nothing very remarkable in all this, your readers will think. But what will they say when I tell them that behind her bed was a fairly large Aron Hakodesh or Ark and by the side of it a Reader's Desk? Such, however, is the fact. The room was not only a kitchen and a bedroom, it was also a *shul* or rather a *chevra*.
>
> It seems that a dozen or so of poor foreigners have clubbed together to form a *minyan*. They subscribe twopence a week and pay the occupier of the house in Hanbury Street where I was visiting two shillings a week for the use of his kitchen as a *Shul*. Relatively to the humble surroundings the Ark looked rather imposing. It only contained a small *Sepher* (and a little religious lumber such as a *Tallis* and an *Aleph Bes* card) but it was large enough to hold two or three scrolls. *Shema Yisroel* in gilt letters were inscribed on the doors and there was a pretty stuff curtain in front. On a piece

of cardboard were inscribed the *Asereth Hadibroth*. The Reader's desk was less pretentious. It was so rickety that one of the occupants of the room humorously remarked 'Don't open the door or you will blow it down.' The slope on which the Reader's book rested was made out of an old lemonade box and covered over with red chintz. The walls were decorated with an *Hanosen Teshuah* in which the name of Kveen Victoria appeared as large as life (yes, our foreign Jews are thoroughly loyal to the queen in whose blessed land they have found an asylum from foreign persecution); a *Mizrach*, a Hebrew memorial inscription and, lastly a dirty photo of Dr Artom. The only other article of furniture connected with the use to which the room is put on Sabbaths stood on the shelf over the fireplace. It was a rough deal box covered outside with wallpaper and inside with red chintz. It contained the prayer-books of the humble congregation – their *Beis Rachel*'s and *Sidurs* and *Chumoshim*. It stood up, and the side fronting the room had been split through, so that it could swing to and fro in folding doors. The fact is that formerly this small box had served to deposit the Sepher Torah in, until somebody had kindly presented them with a proper Ark since when it has been utilised in the way I have described.

I could not refrain from expressing my surprise that people should choose to worship in such a humble apartment when there are so many Chevras in the immediate neighbourhood. I put the question to my Baal Boss: 'Princelet Street Shul is within a stone's throw why not go there?' 'Oh, that's only for rich people,' was his reply, 'and we are poor. If you go there you have to *shnoder* half-a-crown, and a poor man has to wait ever so long before he can get a *Leah*. But here almost everybody can get a *Leah* every Shabbath for nothing. That's why we founded this Chevra. For twopence a week we can have as many *Mitzvahs* as we want.'

His reply set me musing. Here were people so poor that even Princelet Street was too fashionable and expensive for them, and the same motives which induce the foreign Jews to hold aloof from the large city synagogues and found their own Chevras, like those in Princelet Street, Steward Street, and Greenfield Street, were in operation to detach people even from these meeting houses and found something more humble and private still. And what an eloquent proof such an unlooked-for incident furnishes of the profound attachment to their religion which animates the poor foreigners. Some of them can ill afford even twopence a week, but they subscribe it gladly to worship in a kitchen, and would rather put up with all the attendant inconveniences than forego the opportunity of being frequently called to the Law. 'How long have you been in existence?' I asked. 'Nearly two years.' 'Do you meet here on Rosh Hashonah and Yom Kippur also?' 'Yes' was the reply. 'Have you a regular reader?' 'No, anybody can read who likes. Sometimes I *duvan* and sometimes one of the others. If you were to come here one day we might ask you.'

I have not yet availed myself of this kindly offer, but since writing the above, I called one Friday to pay a second visit to my invalid. I found her up and about, though she still retained a few scars. She had a large tub of water by her side with which she was going to scrub the room out in order to prepare it for evening service.

Appendix ii

Hesped by Rabbi Levene on the Death of Rabbi Shmuel Kalman Melnick

Translated from the Hebrew by Ian Melnick

> Rabbi Berachiah said the upper waters and the lower waters were only separated through weeping; 'In tears the rivers were wounded.' Rabbi Tanhuna disagrees with him because of the verse 'He made the earth with his strength . . . with a noise He confused the water.' The word noise refers only to crying, for example 'a voice is heard on high . . . Rachel weeps for her children.'
>
> (Midrash Rabba on Genesis V 4)

In this quotation there is disagreement. According to Rabbi Berachiah the verse is, 'In tears the rivers were wounded,' and Rabbi Tanhuna 'With a noise He confused the water.' In Rabbi Berachiah's opinion only the lower waters cried, not the upper waters as can be seen from his chosen verse because the words 'in tears' refers to deep water i.e. the lower waters. Rabbi Tanhuna suggests both sets, the upper as well as the lower, cried because the verse, 'With a noise He confused the water' refers to heaven. We have to understand why the lower waters cried over this matter. I have seen an explanation by the Maharzov (Rabbi Ze'ev Woolf Heidenheim 1752-1832) on this *midrash*. He quotes a *midrash* on the Psalms which says that before the waters were separated, they were on high with the throne of glory and, subsequently, were limited and lowered. Consequently they cried that they were lowered from heaven and eternity to death and beyond; thus we see that they fell from the high heavens to the depths below so they cried. We find in the *gemara* (Chagiga p.5) that Rabbi (Judah the Prince) took a book of Kinot and reading it reached the verse, 'He cast from the heavens earth, the glory of Israel,' dropped the book and said, 'from the heavens above to the depths below.' It was hard for them to be separated from a place next to eternity to be put amongst death and because of this they cried. This is all very well for the lower waters but why should the upper waters also cry since they remained in their place? The answer is that the upper waters joined and shared the troubles of their brothers; they said woe unto us for our brothers, our flesh with whom we grew up together, how can we see their troubles? how did they fall from the high heavens to the depths below? The lower waters cried more, but the upper waters also cried just as when David's sorrows increased so Jonathan wept for him.

My brothers and friends, don't we all know, unfortunately, the great calamity which has befallen our beloved, that the gift of life has been separated from Harav, Hagaon, Rav Shmuel Kalman; it has come upon us suddenly and frighteningly and the mouth which produced pearls of wisdom has become silent not even speaking during those final hours before the departure of his pure soul. His eyes lit up like stars and watched over his friends and his family, but was not able to say even one word to them. His mouth produced pearls of wisdom, almost all of London heard his Torah and now his soul is resting. Who amongst us did not want to hear from him his final words? but, alas, we have not merited it and Shmuel is dead. Who was able to measure his great pain and bitterness of soul when his eyes watched over everything and he was not able to bless his dearest before his death. It was suddenly felt how he fell from the lofty heavens to the deep abyss. The mouth which spoke great things is now silent. I have heard in the name of the great Gaon the Chidushei Harim an explanation of the verse 'I besought G-d at that time saying. . .' He explains the phrase 'I besought G-d,' as just as he pleaded at that time, he will also plead with G-d at the time of his death, to put it another way the words 'at that time' refer to his death. But, alas, Harav Rav Shmuel Kalman did not give us the merit of allowing us to listen to him before his death. Who was able to measure the greatness of his pain? But, my brothers and friends, we also have to shed tears over this!

How our beloved one who loved every Jewish person and who was always full of happiness and joy, has now gone down from his brothers. He was among the greatest people living and now he has gone down with the dead. Brothers and friends, you still do not know who has gone from us and I have to tell you about his great goodness and, if previously his deeds were unknown, I shall now inform you of them.

In this week's Sidrah (Beshalach, Exodus XIII 17 – XVII 16) is the verse, 'It was when Pharaoh sent out the people. . .' and the *midrash* on it quotes a parable: a man possessed an orchard about which a friend said, 'sell it to me,' so he did so for one *maneh* not knowing its value. When asked how much he had sold it for, he replied 'one *maneh*' to which they replied that it contained olives, grapes, and pomegranates each worth one hundred *manehs*, also various types of spice and other valuable plants each also worth a hundred *manehs*. They went on to tell him that he obviously had no idea what was in that orchard and what he had sold; in fact there were even fields of spikenard and crocuses and if the person had only bought a water fountain even then he would have lost out since it says, 'Garden fountains, a well of running water flowing from Lebanon.' The seller began to regret his action, similarly Pharaoh after sending the people out had nothing left and his chief advisors said to him, 'What have you done?' All they had left was shame on their hands. 'The mixed multitude also went up with them,' that was not all for many rich, wise and skilled people also left with them. 'He sent you an orchard of pomegranates,' at that moment he began to fret and then, 'It was when he sent . . . That is the *midrash*.'

My brothers and friends, the mistake that we have just seen is a mistake that many people make when they have a beautiful article in their possession and don't realise and only get to know of its real value after selling it. Pharaoh didn't know that Israel had brought riches to his land and only realised it after sending them away when the land became as a net without any fish or as a fishpond without weed with the remaining fish departing, therefore Pharaoh cried. We are behaving in exactly the same way at this time concerning a Talmud Chochom who came to England. Who can speak about former years when many tried to take the crown from his head and despise him without knowing what was inside him and without giving him due honour, but how do we look upon him after his departure from this world?

My brothers and friends, the departed of whom we speak was for some time a rabbi living in London, the capital city and how much trouble and difficulties did he put up with, which will bring his soul to its reward and we did not have any feeling for his situation. Shmuel lies in the temple of G-d and now when he has died all Israel gather together to eulogise and to mourn for him.

Brothers and friends, how do we have to cry and shed tears for him because He who sent him sent you an orchard of pomegranates, a man completely immersed in Torah, its services and deeds; woe that he has gone and woe that we have lost him (all cry). And now, my friends, we will seek from the departed that he will give us a good recommendation before our Father in heaven and swallow up death forever. Amen.

Appendix iii

Translation of the Inscription on Rabbi Melnick's Tombstone

Here lies
THE RABBI THE GREAT LUMINARY
THE RIGHTEOUS TEACHER OF LONDON AND RABBI OF MANY CONGREGATIONS
RABBI SHMUEL KALMAN SON OF GERSHON YAAKOV

And Samuel was dead and for him mourned all Israel
Stop and weep over the destruction of the choicest of creation here who has gone down to the grave
They wailed they cried a lament over him for with him died wisdom and understanding
The day you rose from us we gave yea we cried out in eulogy and dirge
A voice from thousands of mouths was heard for removed from us was a beacon among the learned
For this righteous man the teachers of the people mourned with weeping and wailing
The mouth uttered pearls in occupation with Torah day and night
There was nothing left of his pure reverence and scholarship
His shining face and pleasant voice and his hand stretched out to the poor
He was interested in and established peace
He was faithful and beloved by all
The gates of heaven opened and the angels of peace came to meet you rejoicing
A good name for yourself you made   To the house of G-d you did ascend

Born Zakroczym Poland 5622   Died London Shevat 8 5688

May His Soul Be Bound Up In The Bond Of Eternal Life

Appendix iv

Translations of notes found in some of his books
(by Geoffrey Melnick)

1) The Sota 14a tells us that an expedition tried to find the burial place of Moses. The expedition split into two parties, one going to the top of the mountain, the other to the bottom. The party at the top saw the grave at the bottom, the other saw it at the top.
   This seems to confirm the idea that something (totally) spiritual can change its perspective; spiritual things not being governed by normal physical laws. Thus the grave of Moses appears to be in two different places. From this we can understand the statement in the Kedusha of Shabbat and Yom Tov: 'His Glory fills the whole world,' but His ministering angels ask each other, 'Where is the place of His glory?' for each angel sees the place of His glory as elsewhere.
2) The Talmud (Megillah 9b) tells us that meanings of several words in the Torah were changed by the writers of the Septuagint. One of these was *arnevet* [ארנבת] (Lev. XI 6, Deut. XIV 7) one of the forbidden animals since the wife of Ptolemy was named Arnevet. A note added says that elsewhere (beginning of Perek Mi Shemetu) it states that Arnevet was the mother of Ptolemy. [Following the Septuagint the word *arnevet* is usually translated as 'hare' but the description is of an animal that chews the cud whilst not having cloven hooves.]
3) Derech Eretz Zutra p. 123 Rab. Huja taught, 'Silence is good for the wise, how much more so for fools.' The explanation of 'how much more so for fools,' seems to be that if silence is good for the wise it is even more good to have a strict law for fools – to which they probably won't listen anyway.
4) The Talmud (Berakoth 7b) tells us that Rabbi Johanan said (in the name of Rabbi Simeon ben Yohai), 'from the day that the Holy One, blessed be He, created the world there was no man that called Him Lord until Abraham came and called Him Lord.
   Alshich quotes a *Midrash* which says that after Adam had given names to all cattle and other living things the Holy One, blessed be He, said to him 'What is My name?' to which he replied, 'You shall be called Lord of the world.' My humble opinion is that it appears to explain with the aid of the Almighty that Abraham our father did something more than Adam

because when Adam called the Holy One, blessed be He, Lord there was no one else to tell, no-one else other than he and his wife; in fact at the time he named all the animals and the Almighty asked what His name was to be, he didn't even have a wife because only after this is it written, 'And G-d said – it is not good that man should dwell alone, I will make . . .' It was no great thing that Adam knew the Holy One, blessed be He, was Lord over all. But Abraham our father was different. He had had many battles – with his father, with Nimrod and with the people of his land who were immersed in idolatry and served gods of wood and stone. He had great battles with them until he was victorious when they recognised that G-d was indeed G-d and L-rd of all. No one called G-d *Lord* in that way until the coming of Abraham our father, peace be upon him. May G-d forgive us all our sins and remember the covenant with Abraham who gave over his soul for the sake of the Holy One, blessed be He.

This is what is meant here when it says 'till Abraham no-one called the Holy One, blessed be He, Lord.'

5)   The Talmud (Berakoth 60a) tells us that on an occasion Hillel the Elder was returning from a journey when a great tumult was heard coming from the town. He said 'I am sure that does not come from my house.'

The note refers to Avoth d'Rabbi Nathan Chapter 7: 'Let your children be accustomed to humility, how? When a man is humble, his house is also so and he can go abroad and need only pray that his wife doesn't make trouble with the neighbours. But if a man is not humble and his children are arrogant, he prays that both his wife and his children do not make trouble, he remaining uneasy during the whole of his voyage'.

From this I infer that this is why Hillel was so sure that the row wasn't from his house. His humility and greatness were such that they spilled over onto every member of his household. He heard the tumult from the town and knew it was the sound of argument and dispute; he knew it wasn't from his home.

6)   The Talmud (Rosh Hashana 31b) tells us that Rabbi Yochanan ben Zakkai lived 120 years of which 40 years were spent in business, 40 in studying and 40 teaching.

The 40 years in business were certainly before those of learning so at the time he was involved in business he was the same as anyone else. This makes it difficult to understand the Talmud in Succoth 28a which says of Rabbi Yochanan ben Zakkai that never during his life did he utter profane words. Granted that this was true of his periods of study and teaching, what can we say about his years in business except to say that they were not included in the expression 'his life' as were the times that he studied and taught, the period that he engaged in worldly affairs being excluded from this expression. Further Berakoth 61b quotes Rabbi Akiva as saying: 'All my days I have been troubled by the term "and with all your soul" which means even if He takes your soul.' Yet Rabbi Akiva spent his early years as an ignorant shepherd about which he said, 'When I was an ignoramus I said give me a learned man and I will dash his brains out.' At that time he was certainly unable to read the *shema* with understanding. Obviously the term 'my days' is not to be taken literally; it means from the time he returned to the faith as explained regarding Rabbi Yochanan ben Zakkai. Similarly we find that the Talmud in Berakoth says of Rabbi Shimon ben Lakish (Resh Lakish) 'never in his days was his mouth filled with derision as was the case with Rabbi Yochanan ben Zakkai his teacher.' It is impossible to understand the term 'his days' literally since it is well known that Resh Lakish was a robber who returned to the correct way, so it must mean from the time he returned to the faith.

7) Shabbat 118b R. Yochanan said in the name of R Shimon ben Yohai, 'If only Israel would keep two Shabbatot according to *halacha* they would immediately be redeemed.'

It falls to my humble self, with the assistance of the Almighty, to explain the phrase, 'If only Israel would keep two Shabbatot they would immediately be redeemed.' The holy Zohar tells us in numerous places that a Torah Scholar is called 'Shabbat' and just as a weekday prepares for Shabbat so ordinary people are required to provide the needs of the scholar (to allow him to study), e.g. the Zohar instructs us to have a rabbi, paid for by the community to sit and study and teach. The Talmud (Shabbat 119b) says, 'Jerusalem was destroyed because they abused Torah scholars,' also, 'the destruction was because they profaned the Shabbat.' There we have the meaning: If only Israel would observe both types of Shabbat, the Shabbat in memory of creation and the Shabbat of the Torah scholars i.e. honouring both, then Israel would be redeemed immediately.

8) Gittin 7a Mar Ukva sent for advice on how to deal with some people who had set themselves against him {Rashi – they cursed and shamed him}.

It appears that they cursed and shamed Mar Ukva because he had wanted to have relations with a married woman. (According to Rashi in Sanhedran 31b quoting an *agadah* Mar Ukva was a *Baal teshuva* who had taken a liking to a certain woman but had subsequently left her and she married another. Later, after he fell ill, she had to come to him to borrow money. Despite himself he fell in love with her but managed to conquer his desires, she left in peace and he recovered.) Presumably it was because of this incident that these sinners and evil men shamed and cursed him, failing to judge him in the scale of merit.

9) Succah 28a 'They said of Rabbi Yochanan ben Zakkai that he did not leave unstudied . . . {numerous texts} . . . and the speech of palm trees.' The Tosephot on Menahot 71a explains that date palms are dioecious and it was common practice to graft male branches onto female trees. It may be this is only done in the case of palm trees which are easily lost that one is allowed to graft throughout *erev* Pesach. As the Mishna states, 'Just as the [date] palm tree has a desire [for a male tree] so do Israel have a desire to do the will of their father in Heaven.' The Talmud elsewhere discusses palm trees in Jericho about which it is told – a certain person saw a palm tree and understood it desired a mate. He told the palm trees in Jericho what it wanted and brought a branch from there and grafted it on from when the tree produced fruit as it had done before.

10) Succah 45b 'Happy are they who wait for Him (Hebrew לו lo). The numerical value of the word *lo* is 36. It seems to me that the form of the marriage blessing: 'Who created man in His image, in the image of His likeness and has prepared for him (*lo*) an everlasting house . . .' This can be explained as follows – according to the Midrash (on Ki Thissa) all the souls that were and will be throughout the world come directly from Adam, so the thirty-six righteous in every generation who are the foundations of the world and through whom the Messiah will come (speedily in our days) also are derived from Adam. This is, 'He decreed *lo* for Himself. He decreed the thirty-six from Himself as an everlasting house.'

11) Sanhedrin 56b An authority is quoted as saying that Rav Hidka is quoted only once in the Talmud in Shabbat 117b where he states that on Shabbat one is required to have four meals compared to the others who say only three. In that case he takes part in a detailed discussion, here he only makes a short statement.

In Avoth d'Rabi Nathan p.77 'Elisha ben Avuya says' he was the 'other' spoken of in Hagiga as the learned rabbi who became a heretic no longer keeping the Torah but an incident is recalled in the Tosephot to Hagiga 16a which says that he repented at the end of his life. Therefore his penitence was accepted and he merited to have Torah spoken in his name.

12) This appeared as Chapter 29 of *Sepher Mareh Cohain* by Menaseh Adler (Hacohen), London 5679 (1919). It seems to have been written by Rabbi Melnick especially for the book.

(Translation from the Hebrew by Ian Melnick)

To honour my friend the rabbi, great in Torah and its observance – Rabbi Shmuel Kalman Melinek

Concerning the question raised by the Maharsha [Rabbi Shmuel Edels 1555-1631] about the incident described in Ketuvoth 67b over which Mar Ukva doubles the amount he sends to a poor man. The Maharsha asks how the poor man could have been allowed to accept an extra four hundred *zuzim*, to which one might answer by saying that Mar Ukva's son did not actually give the money to him since after seeing the man with some wine he returned to his father with the money. However this answer is not valid as the son must have handed the money over. Both stories about Mar Ukva have some element of secrecy to them; the first one is the story of him pushing four *zuzim* through the door so as not to embarrass the poor man. The Talmud (Bava Basra 10a), the Rambam and Shulchan Aruch attribute this good characteristic to Mar Ukva as that was his normal way of giving charity and there was only one accident.

For the second case he changes from his norm to send the money publicly; this time he sends it by his son publicly. We have to understand that the second case deals with a respectable poor person who does not want to live off charity. Such a person is considered an *armuh* and should be supported either by presents or by loans as described in Yoreh Deah 213, 9 (source is Ketuvoth 67b). Therefore Mar Ukva had to support him publicly by giving presents rather than secretly by pushing money through his door as even that would not have been accepted. He would only accept it as an *armuh* by means of a present.

With this idea we can answer the question of the Maharsha: *erev* Yom Kippur is a day of good will, a day for good deeds and giving a present is an honourable thing, therefore he chose that day to give his present. When his son saw wine being poured for the poor man he told his father that he didn't need the money. From that moment the intention behind the donation was not necessarily as a present as he was no longer a poor man. However at that particular time the son had to leave the money with him and could not return it as we read in Yoreh Deah 258, 6 and in Pithhe Yeshurah [a commentary on Shulchan Aruch by Rabbi Abraham Eisenstadt 1812-1868] which quotes a responsum of the Penei Aryeh who says that if someone entrusts someone else to deliver a present, the present must be delivered and may not be returned. Anyway it is clear that it may not be returned and he had to give the present to the poor man. The question of the Maharsha about how could the poor man who already had two hundred *zuzim* accept any more still stands. According to the way I have explained the problem you can answer that Mar Ukva was not giving charity to a poor man but a present to an *armuh* and in such a case even more than two hundred *zuzim* is perfectly acceptable as is seen in Yoreh Deah 253, in the Ramoh and in Pithhe Teshuvah in the name of the Radbaz. I conclude with the blessing of his friend Menasseh Adler Hacohen.

(An incomplete note to the same effect and in almost the same words appears as a margin note on the relevant page of Rabbi Melnick's copy of the Talmud.)

Appendix v

PRINCELET STREET SYNAGOGUE
MILE END NEW TOWN SYNAGOGUE

MARCH 1952

SCHEME FOR PROPOSED MERGER

NAME.—The proposed name shall be the joint one of "PRINCELET STREET AND MILE END NEW TOWN SYNAGOGUE."

TRUSTEESHIP.—There will be four trustees of whom two shall be appointed by Princelet Street, and two by Mile End New Town.

PROPERTY.—Both the Leasehold property at 19 Princelet Street, and the freehold property at No. 39 Dunk Street, London, E.1, shall be held jointly by all four trustees under a suitable Trust Deed to be prepared by Solicitors.

BANK AND INVESTMENT ACCOUNTS.—

(a) Mile End New Town will transfer its Current Account and Investment Deposit Account to the Princelet Street Current Account (with Barclays Bank Ltd.) and to the Princelet Street Deposit Account (with the London Savings Bank).

(b) Both Current and Deposit Accounts shall be controlled by three signatories of which two shall be persons authorised by Princelet Street members and one by Mile End New Town members.

SILVER, VESTMENTS, SCROLLS, FURNITURE and other Assets.—These will be transferred to the Princelet Street premises.

SUBSCRIPTION.—Until further arrangements can be made, the weekly rates paid by members of each congregation shall remain unchanged.

RIGHTS.—The Membership and Funeral Rights of members in each congregation shall be unaffected. Upon the merger and entry into Princelet Street, members of Mile End New Town shall have the same rights, privileges, advantages, seating facilities and responsibilities as those of Princelet Street members (except only in the differences in payment of weekly subscriptions).

HON. OFFICERS AND COMMITTEE.—Each congregation shall retain its existing Honorary Officers and Committee, who shall continue to function side by side and administer the affairs of both congregations for a period of 12 months after the date of merger, and until then, the Hon. Treasurers of both congregations shall be Joint Hon. Treasurers. At the expiration of this period only one set of Hon. Officers and one Committee shall, however, be elected to office upon an Annual General Meeting to be convened, in which fully paid-up members of both congregations shall enjoy complete voting rights in the election.

PAID OFFICERS.

1. **Mile End New Town.**

    (a) **S. Abramovitch** (Beadle). The joint congregations shall continue to maintain and pay his weekly pension of 15s. for life.

    (b) **H. Kushin** (Collector). His services shall be retained for a period of 12 months from the date of merger, as collector for this period only of Mile End New Town Members. Subscriptions on the same terms as have prevailed hitherto.

2. **Princelet Street.**

    (a) **Secretary.** Mr. S. Reback (Jnr.) shall retire.

    (b) **Collector and Beadle.** Mr. M. Reback (Senr.) shall continue his employment on the regular staff.

    (c) **Minister.** Rev. N. Caplan shall continue his present employment on the regular staff.

    (d) **Generally.** No paid official shall be called upon to retire annually.

FEDERATION OF SYNAGOGUES.—The proposed merger shall be subject to the formal consent of the Federation of Synagogues.

Appendix vi

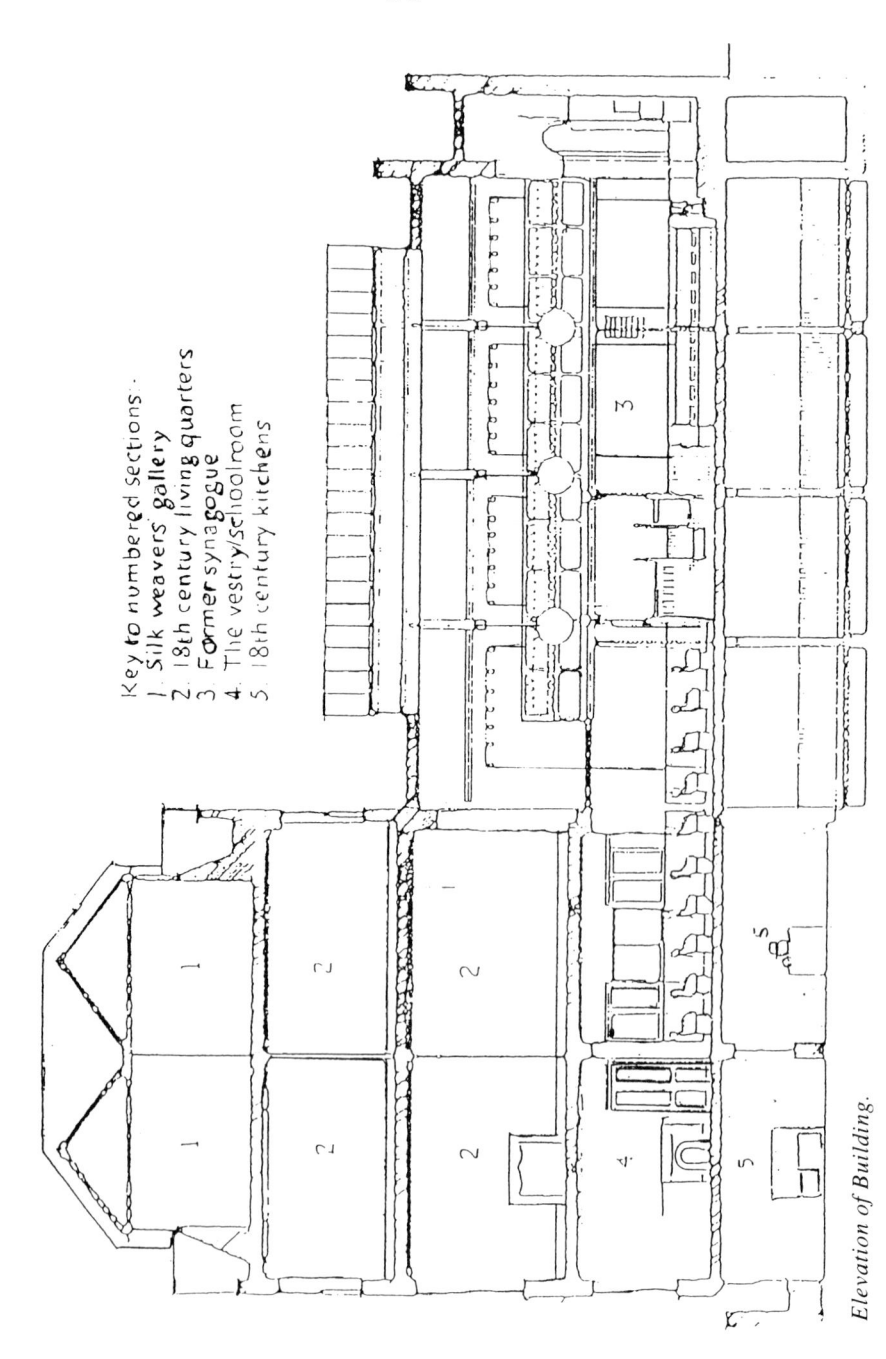

Key to numbered sections:
1. Silk weavers gallery
2. 18th century living quarters
3. Former synagogue
4. The vestry/schoolroom
5. 18th century kitchens

Elevation of Building.

Appendix vii

Appeal for Funds
for the
Partial Rebuilding
of the
Princes Street Synagogue

This Synagogue, likewise connected with a Provident Society, which provides for its Members in sickness and shiva, and pays for the burial of Members and relieves them in distress, has been established a quarter of a century. The Lease having recently expired, the Committee were successful in obtaining a renewal of the same for a term of 50 years.

Many structural alterations became necessary, and the Hon Architect to the Federation, Mr L Solomons, was instructed to report on the condition of the present building. In his report several portions were condemned, the roof is in a dangerous condition, and ingress and egress is not sufficient.

This Synagogue is situated in a densely populated locality of the poorest Jewish inhabitants, and is always well attended. The Committee find themselves unable to carry out the necessary improvements unaided, and they, therefore, appeal for assistance to carry out the proposed alterations which will cost about £500.

Donations will be thankfully received, and acknowledged by the following gentlemen;

Rev Dr Adler, Chief Rabbi,
22, Finsbury Square, E.C.
Samuel Montagu, Esq, M.P.
60, Old Broad Street, E.C.
J Davidson Esq, President of the Princes St Synagogue,
16, Princes Street, Spitalfields, E.
M Joel, Esq, Warden,
61 Great Prescot Street, E

Appeal 1892/3.

Glossary

Adon Olum	Sovereign of the Universe. Poem at beginning of the Morning Service, sung as hymn at end of Shabbat, Festival and special services.
Agadah	Legends and tales in the Talmud, etc., cf. *halacha*.
Aleph Bes	Hebrew alphabet
Amidah	Prayer said silently while standing facing an easterly direction or, in synagogue, the Ark. There are different versions for weekdays, Shabbat, Festivals, etc.
Asereth Hadibroth	Ten Commandments.
Ashkenazi	Pertaining to Jews from Germany, Poland and other parts of Northern Europe (pl. Ashkenazim), cf. *Sephardi*.
Baal Boss	Corruption of Baal Habeiyis – Master of the household.
Baal Musaph	One who reads the Additional Service of Shabbat and Festival.
Baal Shacharis	One who reads the Morning Service of Shabbat and Festival.
Baal Teshuva	A repentant.
Barmitzvah	Coming of age of a boy at 13.
Beis Rachel	Book read by women in Eastern Europe during the synagogue service.
Berakhoth	Blessings.
Beth Din	Religious court of Law consisting of at least three members.

Beth Hamedrash	Study Centre doubling as synagogue.
Bikur Cholim	Visiting the sick.
Bimah	Platform for the reader in the synagogue.
Boruch Habo	Blessed is he who comes. Welcome to an important visitor.
Chanukah	Eight day festival commemorating the defeat of the Greeks by the Hasmoneans 165 BCE.
Chassidim	Religious movement, originating in Eastern Europe in second half of eighteenth century, in which fervent piety is based on mysticism; led by hereditary spiritual leaders.
Chazan	Synagogue reader or cantor.
Chevra	A society or club for religious purposes.
Chevra Ahavath Torah	Society of Lovers of the Torah.
Chosan	Bridegroom.
Chosan Bereshis	Bridegroom of the Beginning, the person called to the Torah on Simchas Torah for the reading of the first chapter of the Torah.
Chosan Torah	Bridegroom of the Torah, the person called to the reading of the last portion of the Torah on Simchas Torah.
Chullin	Book of the Mishnah.
Chumash	Book of the Pentateuch, usually also contains the relevant Haphtorah portions, *v.i.*
Chupah	The canopy beneath which the bride and bridegroom are ceremonially married.
Dayan	Ecclesiastical judge, member of a *Beth Din*, *v.s.*
Drosha	Sermon.
Duvan	Say prayers.
Fane	Archaic or poetic term for any sacred building.
Gemara	See *Talmud*.
Gemilloth Chassodim	Performing acts of kindness of a charitable nature.
Hagaon	A great rabbinic scholar.
Halacha	The entire body of Jewish religious law (adj. *halachic*).
Hanosen Teshuah	Prayer for the government of the country; in England the Sovereign and Royal Family.
Haphtorah	Portion from the Prophets read after the week's Torah portion.

Havdalah	Ceremony to mark the termination of Shabbat or Festival.
Hesped	Eulogy.
Hillel	Prominent scholar at time of second Temple. On an occasion as a student and unable to afford the tuition fee he climbed the building and listened to the lecture through the skylight. It was winter, it snowed and he nearly froze to death.
Jahrzeit	Anniversary of the death of a person.
Kaddish	Prayer in praise of G-d read at certain points in the regular services and also said by mourners during the eleven months following the death of a parent and on the *jahrzeit*.
Kashrus	The observance of the dietary laws and the supervision of the necessary arrangements.
Kedusha	Special prayer read during the repetition of the *Amidah* by the *chazan* recalling the vision of Isaiah on receiving his call to be a prophet.
Kesubah	Marriage contract.
Kinot	Collection of mourning poems and prose read on the anniversary of the destruction of the Temples.
Kupple	Skull cap.
Leah	Corruption of *Aliyah*, the honour of being called to the reading of a portion from the week's *sedrah*.
Maggid	Preacher.
Maneh	A large value coin.
Megillah	Book of Esther, also used for books of Ruth, Song of Songs, Ecclesiastes, Lamentations.
Menorah	Eight-branched candelabrum used for Chanukah v.s.
Midrash Rabba	Compilation of homiletical utterances used to explain points in the Torah and/or drive home a moral or religious lesson.
Minyan	Quorum of ten males of the age of thirteen and above required for a full service.
Mikdash Me'at	Any synagogue, being of lesser status than the Temple in Jerusalem.

Mizrach	(Lit. East) A device to indicate the eastern wall in a house to signify the correct direction to turn during the *Amidah* prayer.
Mitzvah	A religious obligation.
Musaph	Additional service on Shabbat and Festival days.
Mohel	One who performs religious circumcision.
Ner Tamid	Perpetual light in synagogue.
Oleinu	Prayer said at end of all services, followed by mourner's *Kaddish*, v.s.
Peroches	Curtain covering the Ark in the synagogue.
Pesach	Passover.
Purim	Minor festival commemorating the events described in the *Megillah*.
Rambam	Rabbi Moshe ben Maimon, Maimonides (1135-1204). Scholar, rabbi and physician. Born in Spain but lived in Egypt where he was a physician to the royal household.
Rashi	Rabbi Shimon ben Yitzchok (1040-1105). Noted commentator on Bible and Talmud. Lived in France.
Rav	Rabbi, spiritual head of a congregation.
Rebbe	Spiritual leader of a chassidic sect.
Rosh Hashanah	New Year Festival.
Rosh Hashochetim	Head of the *shochetim*, v.i.
Seder Service	Home service on first nights of Pesach.
Sedra	Weekly portion from the Torah.
Semicha	Qualification to be a rabbi.
Sephardi	Pertaining to Jews originating from Spain and Portugal, cf. *Ashkenazi*. (pl. *Sephardim*).
Sephardish	Rite of certain Ashkenazi Jews similar to that of the Sephardim.
Sepher Torah	Scroll of the Torah. The most holy item in the possession of modern Jews. (pl. *Sifrei Torah*).
Seuda Shelishit	A special third meal eaten on Shabbat.
Shabbat	Sabbath day.
Shabbat Hagadol	The Sabbath prior to Pesach.
Shabbat Shuva	The Sabbath between Rosh Hashanah and Yom Kippur.
Shabbat Zachor	The Sabbath prior to Purim.
Shammas	Synagogue beadle.

Shavuot	Feast of Weeks; Pentecost.
Shechita	Method of ritual slaughter for Jewish food.
Shema	Most important prayer consisting of Deuteronomy VI 4-9, XI 13-21, Numbers XV 37-41.
Shema Yisroel	First words of the Shema: 'Hear O Israel'.
Shemini Atzereth	Festival at end of Succoth.
Shiurim	Lessons on any religious subject. (sing. *Shiur*).
Shiva	Week of confined mourning following burial of a close relative.
Shnoder	A voluntary charitable offering usually following an *Aliyah*.
Shochet	One who performs *shechita*. (pl. *Shochetim*).
Shofar	Ram's horn sounded on Rosh Hashanah.
Shomer	Supervisor ensuring food preparation is in conformity with laws of *kashrus*. (pl. *Shomerim*).
Shool	Synagogue.
Shul	Spelling variant of *shool*.
Shulchan Aruch	Codified form of religious laws.
Siddur	Prayer book. (pl. *Siddurim*).
Simchat Torah	Final day of the Succoth Festival during which the annual reading of the Torah is completed.
Siyum	Celebration on completion of the study of any book of the Talmud.
Siyum Hatorah	Celebration on completion of the study of the entire Talmud.
Sopher	Scribe.
Stiebel	Small synagogue usually of a chassidic sect.
Stille Chasenes	Marriage ceremonies valid according to Jewish law but not registered according to English law and without the authority of the Chief Rabbi.
Succoth	Festival of Tabernacles.
Tallis	Four-cornered garment with a tassel at each corner worn during reading of prayers. (pl. *Tallesos*, col. *Tallesim*).
Talmud	Classic collection of rabbinic law and commentary, recording legal decisions and discussions, from about 200 BCE to 450 CE. Consists of two parts – *Mishna* and *Gemara*.
Talmud Torah	(lit. Study of Torah) Religious elementary school.

Tehillim	Psalms.
Tephillin	Boxes containing biblical quotations, Exodus XIII 1-10; XI 16; Deuteronomy VI, 4-9; XI 13-21. Worn during weekday morning services strapped on the arm and the head.
Tochecho	Curses if Torah laws are not followed, detailed in Leviticus XXVI 14-45 and Deuteronomy XXVIII 15-68.
Torah	Five books of Moses, the Pentateuch. Also used for the entire gamut of Jewish religious literature.
Tosephet	Running commentary on the Talmud by medieval French, German and Spanish scholars.
Yeshivah	College for Jewish religious studies, especially the Talmud. Often involving a residential requirement (pl *Yeshivos*).
Yiddish	Language of Ashkenazi Jews consisting mainly of high German with Hebrew together with elements of other languages.
Yigdal	'Let us magnify': Poem based on the thirteen principles of faith enunciated by Maimonides forming part of the early morning prayers and sung antiphonally by *chazan* and congregation at end of Shabbat and Festival evening services.
Yom Kippur	Day of Atonement.
Zuzim	Coins of very low value. (sing. *Zuz*).
בעל קורא	*Baal Koreh*. One who reads the week's portion from the Torah.
זצ"ל	Of righteous and blessed memory (formula added to the names of the pious dead).
חזן	*Chazan, v.s.*